Delme

The Autobiography

Dedicated to the memory of
Howard 'Ash' Davies

Delme

The Autobiography

Delme Thomas
with Alun Gibbard

The publishers wish to acknowledge the support of
Cyngor Llyfrau Cymru

Cover design: Y Lolfa
Cover photograph: Emyr Young

ISBN: 978 184771 958 4

Published and printed in Wales
on paper from well-maintained forests by
Y Lolfa Cyf., Talybont, Ceredigion SY24 5HE
website www.ylolfa.com
e-mail ylolfa@ylolfa.com
tel 01970 832 304
fax 832 782

Contents

1

Caravan

WHAT DO YOU do with yourself when you've finished playing first-class rugby? Where does your life go when something that filled it for so long disappears for good?

These questions came into my mind almost as soon as I decided to hang up my boots after 15 years of playing rugby for my club, my country and the British and Irish Lions. When I finished playing in 1974, there wasn't any sort of preparation to help you face the world after rugby, the world you'd be living day in, day out. Doubtless no-one thought that this was necessary because we were, after all, amateur players: we had day jobs which would sustain us once the playing stopped. Our families would still be there, too.

So, it was assumed that work and family commitments would pick up any slack left by rugby's absence. I'm sure that as far as those running the game were concerned, our lives would continue as normal, with no need to think about how well players were coping with missing the game. After all, the only change in our lives would be no need to turn up for training and matches any longer. Life went on as usual, or so everybody thought.

But, for many of us in those days, and certainly for me, rugby was so much more than something we did after work and at weekends. In any one season we could play up to 50 club games, training twice weekly for about ten months, spending the equivalent of a day or so together each week. Then there was our time together in the Five Nations, as international players in the Wales camp, and the tours abroad under the banner of the British Lions. When I played for the Lions we were away from home for months on end. Therefore, as teams – wearing whichever colour – we were together for a considerable time. In such circumstances, a bond builds up between players, which doesn't happen in many other circumstances. It may well be a cliché, but you did become a family. Leaving that family, in my case, Llanelli, proved to be a traumatic experience. It affected my health. It affected my whole personality. Something had been taken away and it left a huge gap in my life. I wasn't ready for it, and it hit me really hard.

Life was pretty good in the first year after finishing playing rugby, though. One significant and positive change in our life as a family was that for the first time I could go on holiday with my wife, Bethan, and our daughters, Tracy and Helen. As a player, any annual leave from work had to be used to go on rugby tours with either Llanelli, Wales or the Lions. My first tour with the Lions had lasted five months. Well, that used up all my annual leave, and a lot more, of course! So to have time off from my job and spend it with my family was a wonderful change. We were able to go to places like Spain and Portugal, just like other families did. We had a caravan at Amroth, Pembrokeshire, as well, which meant weekend breaks away and longer stays during the school holidays. Bethan and I could also go away, just the two of us.

But, however correct the decision I made to end my rugby career, and however enjoyable and fulfilling these new opportunities with my family were, I still didn't anticipate feeling the way I did after finishing playing. Of course, it was the end of an era for Bethan, too. She had been as much a part of the social scene of the rugby club as I had, and now that was gone for her, too.

In those days there were no testimonial matches at the end of a career. I'm not saying for one second that I should have had one, and I don't regret not having one because of the money. No, my point is that having the testimonial game would have marked the end of my playing days properly. It would have brought things to a close in a neater and maybe more definite way.

* * *

Suffice to say that due to the huge gap in my life after my playing days were over, by the beginning of the 1980s things had gone from bad to worse for me personally. I suffered a nervous breakdown.

I was admitted to hospital and stayed there for weeks because my feelings had sunk so low. One thing that's clear to me now, looking back at such a difficult period in my life, is the fact that I didn't want to *admit* that I was in the state I was in. And I don't mean that I just didn't want to admit it to other people, I didn't want to admit it to myself, either. It was extremely difficult to concede to yourself that you were suffering because, quite simply, it would be considered a weakness.

When I ended up in hospital, I hated the fact that I'd been admitted there for such a reason – a mental one, not a physical one. Such an attitude, of course, soon turned out to be a part of the problem, which in turn made things even worse. I refused to accept that I was in the psychiatric ward of a hospital. It would have been far easier for me to come to terms with being a patient on one of the other wards, the ones where patients had illnesses you could see, or understand, at least – illnesses that other people were also far readier to accept. I can see quite clearly now that the biggest mistake people make with any sickness of the mind or emotions, is refusing to accept that you have it in the first place. It makes things a lot worse. Accepting your condition, above all else, allows you to go for the necessary help sooner rather than later.

You see by the early 1980s I'd got to the point where I'd lost interest in life completely. I didn't want to see anyone or go anywhere. I'm sure it wasn't easy to live with someone who felt like this, day in, day out. Thank goodness that Bethan could see what was happening and persevered in telling me that I needed help. That was such an essential part of the road in getting me to seek medical advice in the first place. But, of course, that final step across the threshold of the ward wouldn't happen until I was ready to admit to my condition.

So, what was pressing down on me so heavily that it stopped me facing up to how I really felt? I was worried about what other people would think of me: what was someone who'd been involved so successfully in the world of rugby now doing lying in a hospital bed, in a psychiatric ward. I wasn't much of a British Lion in there, was I?

There's no doubt that I'd let things go on for far too long before agreeing to ask for help from my doctor. As a result, by the time I got to the hospital, I was in a bad way. I couldn't face seeing anyone because I knew that would mean having to answer questions that I didn't want to answer. It's for that same reason that I didn't want to leave the safety and comfort of the hospital ward, later.

Lying in that bed, those thoughts of how others would react to me, an international rugby player laid low by a breakdown, mingled with other far stronger thoughts: I felt that I'd let my family down; I'd failed as far as they were concerned; I'd failed as a father and a husband. That pressure was unbearable.

One thing that did make it more difficult for me, in particular, was the fact that everybody knew who I was. The staff on the ward knew, the other patients knew, and their visitors had heard of me. There was no hiding place; no opportunity to be anonymous. It was difficult to deal with some of the people who came to see me, because they reminded me of the world I was missing. Some who were there to see members of their own families would also pop in to see me sometimes. I knew some, but not all. As kind and as thoughtful as these people were, I'm not sure that I received them as politely and sociably as I'd do so now. Whatever their good intentions, seeing people wasn't something I welcomed at that time.

Two prominent Welshmen were on the same ward as me, Eic Davies and Ronnie Williams. Eic was the man who'd done much to pioneer Welsh-language rugby broadcasting and he was the father of rugby presenter, Huw Llewelyn Davies. Huw came in to see his father regularly and I'd see him now and again. Ronnie was the other half of Ryan and Ronnie, the extremely popular comedy and singing duo. Ryan Davies had died some five years previously. Maybe losing his professional partner had left Ronnie a little directionless, too.

A regular visitor to the ward was one of the hospital chaplains. He was the minister of a chapel in Carmarthen and a former teacher at the grammar school in the town. Glyndwr Walker had taught Ray Gravell and it was my former playing colleague who introduced me to Glyndwr. Grav used to come to visit me regularly and he was at my bedside one day when Glyndwr happened to walk into the ward. Grav shouted across to him, and he came towards us. From that day on, Glyndwr Walker came to see me every single day I was in hospital. We'd have chats about all sorts of things, most of which were of no consequence at all. The important thing was that he visited me regularly, giving me an opportunity to talk. Now and again, he'd grab hold of my hand and that would give me huge encouragement. At other times, he'd say a little prayer, only a few words, but that was of great comfort, too.

While in my hospital bed, I was given news that hit me really hard. Bethan told me that my stepfather had had a heart attack and had passed away. Hearing that news was a severe blow. He'd been the head of our household since I was a very small boy and we'd always got on very well. Now he was gone, and I was lying in a hospital bed suffering from depression. I can't say what effect that had on me or how I felt on the day of the funeral. I was given permission to leave hospital to go to the burial, but I had to be back in my bed that evening. I'd never experienced such feelings in my life before and, thank goodness, I've never experienced anything like that since.

When I was in hospital I wasn't restricted to my bed, so one day Glyndwr took me to the hospital chapel. We both sat there talking to each other quietly for about ten minutes. Nearly every day afterwards I'd go back there, with Glyndwr at first, but then on my own. Sitting in that chapel was a big help. It's very difficult to explain why, but it did start to make me feel better about myself.

One day when I went to the chapel the door was

locked. When Glyndwr asked me later that day if I'd been to the chapel, I explained to him that I couldn't, and why. He wasn't happy to hear that, as the chapel should be open at all times. He went to find out why and learned that some patients had been going in there to use their phone when they shouldn't. As a result, the chapel had been locked. From that day on, Glyndwr would personally take me down to the chapel. I was so glad that those visits didn't come to an end. Belief and faith became integral partners in lifting me out of the situation that had put me in hospital in the first place. When I was allowed to leave hospital, I was still unable to go back to my job. I was off work for about six months in total, before my life started to pull itself back together again. It took over a year, however, before I was back to anything like I was before the illness.

Chapel values have been very important to me since the Sunday school days of my upbringing. Due to the pressures of playing first-class rugby on Saturdays, I'd stopped going to chapel because I wanted to spend as much time as I could with my family at the weekend. However, after my experience in the hospital, I started attending chapel regularly, the chapel I used to go to when I was a child, in Bancyfelin, where I was born. Glyndwr would continue to call to see me at home about once a week. He gave me his phone number and insisted that I ring him if I needed him, any time of the day. I had very special care and support from him.

There are still some days when I feel low in spirits

and I don't feel quite as I should. But I've learned how to deal with that now. I don't hide behind it and I don't refuse to accept how I feel. I don't deny my feelings any more. When I realise that I'm not feeling right, I go out of the house and mix with people, instead of keeping myself to myself as I used to do. I'll go for a walk, or into Carmarthen. And the caravan at Amroth is a great help at such low times. I find being out in the garden is good medicine too, in the fresh air, doing physical work. I help a friend of mine fairly regularly and we both tend the garden of an elderly lady who goes to the same chapel as me in Bancyfelin.

I believe that it's very important to keep the body fit and healthy for the benefit of one's general well-being, not just physical health. I still have the weights' bar that I had when I was a schoolboy in Bancyfelin and I lift some weights every day for a few minutes. The only mark left by my illness is that I don't like walking into a room full of strangers on my own. That wasn't the case before. The lack of confidence or perhaps shyness, because of my illness, shows itself in that way. But I can deal with that.

I'm very glad – and grateful – that I was never one to drink a lot. I hardly ever drank, not even on the long rugby tours abroad. That might surprise a few! It wasn't as if there was pressure to drink a lot in those days. That also might surprise a few people! I often wonder what would have happened to me had I turned to the bottle at my low points. I'm sure that many who drink heavily do so in order to hide some feelings of depression, feelings they refuse to acknowledge. There's no shame in feeling depressed. The weakness lies in failing to acknowledge it.

This possibly may not be the beginning you expected to the story of someone who was part of the Welsh rugby way of life for a good 15 years. But, this is where I am now, and I suppose it goes to show that we are after all – club members, internationals, and Lions alike – rugby players with feet of clay and hearts of flesh.

2

Number 14

THE GUNS OF the Second World War had started firing and German bombs had fallen on Swansea when I came into this world. But not many people in Bancyfelin would have been *that* aware of the war. The village is tucked away in a quiet corner of rural Carmarthenshire, about five miles from the town that gives the county its name. I was born in 1942, in a place that, as you may know, is very close to my heart. I'm one of five children, with two brothers and two sisters.

My first home was a small cottage on the main road, my grandparents' house on my mother's side, Number 14, Bancyfelin. Everyone knew me as one of Number 14's children. Even today, my brother is known as Dai 14. The cottage was two doors down from the Fox and Hounds pub in the heart of the village. In that same pub, Wales and British Lions centre, Jonathan Davies, was raised. That's why he's nicknamed 'Foxy'.

Three generations of my family lived in Number 14 – my grandparents, my mother and the children. My father had left very early on in my life and I don't want to dwell on that part of the story, for the sake of my family. What's important to me, more than anything else, is that we children were largely raised by our grandparents, and that my mother lived with us. So I was thoroughly spoilt throughout my childhood and have no cause for complaint at all!

My grandfather was a ganger working on the railway tracks. I had many uncles who worked as train drivers on the railways also. My mother was one of eight children, and her family's roots were deep in the Bancyfelin soil. As an adult she had no option but to stay in the village to work, as did most of her siblings. Only one, Uncle Glyn, left the village to pursue a university education and he'll appear in my story later on, as will my Uncle Vincent who ended up living in Australia. Our family history was similar to the story of almost every other family in the village at the time: Welsh in terms of language and heritage, and, like the rest of the children in the village, I couldn't speak a word of English until I was about ten years old. And, despite the fact that it might sound like a rosy cliché, we didn't lock the doors of our houses. We were in and out of each other's homes all the time.

It was – and still largely is – an agricultural area. Helping local farmers at specific times of the year was an exiting activity for children like me who hadn't been brought up on a farm. We'd help with tending sheep and cattle, and at the busy period of haymaking. Everyone had to pull together to make the farms work; if the farms survived, then so did the village.

I spent a great deal of my time on one farm in particular, Castell y Waun. That's where I'd go in the evening and at weekends. When I left school I worked on that farm for over a year and a half. I'm sure that I would've been a farmer if things hadn't turned out the way they did. I enjoyed working with the livestock more than anything else, and I still enjoy going to local agricultural shows today.

Hunting was another aspect of country life that caught my imagination early on. My grandfather would take me hunting for rabbits and wood pigeons. The rabbit was an important part of our family life, as it was to other families in the village at that time, as many meals were based on it. The irony was that we couldn't afford to buy beef very often, despite being surrounded by beef farms. Chicken was certainly not the option it is today to many. The only time we'd have chicken was on Christmas Day and that was because we couldn't afford a turkey.

The Christmas chicken was an absolute treat, I must say. We had chickens at the bottom of the garden though, but they were kept for eggs. Sharing the bottom of our garden with the feathered friends was a pig. Again, nearly every garden in the village had a pigsty. A pig was a useful animal to keep because, once slaughtered, every single part of it could be used for various purposes. Pig's meat was, therefore, readily available to us throughout the year. All this might sound a bit strange and unfamiliar today, but that's what life was like for us in the 1940s and 1950s in Bancyfelin. It was very much closer to the soil, and closer to the rhythms of nature.

The Second World War was the backdrop to the first few years of my life. As I said, we didn't know a great deal about the war in the village – it didn't really touch us. The strongest recollection I do have is of the blackouts. For a child, being suddenly immersed in darkness was something very dramatic. I can clearly remember my grandmother pulling the window blinds down at certain times. Later, I remember some of my uncles returning from the fighting. But that's about it. That was my Second World War.

I have a far clearer and stronger recollection of the long snowfall of 1947. Literally everything came to a complete stop. We couldn't leave our village by car at all, and no-one could visit the place because the roads were blocked. It's strange now, looking back at that time, thinking how people managed to keep going through such extreme circumstances. Snow settled everywhere and drifted to form snow banks of great height, over half the height of many houses. It was certainly a challenge to carry on with life in such circumstances. We had to walk through snow for three miles or so to get to St Clears to fetch bread.

We didn't have water or electricity in the house. Water was carried in buckets from a pump at the top end of the village, and there was another one at the bottom end. My grandmother usually did the carrying in our family. Fetching water was heavy work at the best of times, but doing so in thick snow was even more of an ordeal. Baths were taken in a big zinc tub in front of the fire. Our toilet was at the bottom of the garden, near the chicken coop and pigsty. We'd try to make sure that we coordinated going to the toilet with feeding the chickens, to save us going out too often in the cold and dark.

Electricity came to the village at the beginning of the 1950s, when I wasn't far off ten years old. Prior to that heat for the house came from the coal fire that roared on the hearth, day in, day out. In summer, we children would collect firewood ready for the winter months and this would be mixed with coal to ensure a long-lasting fire. There was always a pile of firewood and larger wooden blocks stacked at the side of the house. Throughout the winter, we'd place thick heavy overcoats at the bottom of living room and bedroom doors in order to keep draughts out.

It was pure joy sitting in front of the fire holding a piece of bread to the flames so that we could have some toast. And it was extra fun if the piece of bread fell into the ashes and we had to start all over again! As children, of course, we weren't aware of the need to count slices of bread at a time of austerity, but the adults rarely showed concern. They just allowed us to be children.

Light in our house came from an oil lamp, the Tilley; well, that was true downstairs, at least. Upstairs we used candles to light the bedroom when we changed to go to bed. At that time there was no other reason to light a bedroom. There were three beds in the room. Three brothers slept in one, two sleeping at the top end of the bed and the other at the bottom. My two sisters were in the second bed and my parents slept in the third.

There was only one car in the village, owned by Sam Jones who kept the garage. He was a very generous person, who made his car available to anyone who lived in Bancyfelin if there was an emergency of some sort.

You may be getting quite a clear picture of village life in my childhood days by now, of everyone pulling together to keep things going. It strikes me now, writing it on paper, that I might be in danger of creating the impression of some idealised world and romanticising the past. But, to be perfectly truthful, that's exactly how people lived and worked together in those days. It's so different to how things are now; we could easily think that the past was actually make-believe. But it wasn't.

Getting half a crown from my mam once or twice a year, so that I could go to the pictures, was an extra special treat. The bus cost a shilling, so too entry to the cinema, which meant that I had enough money left to buy sixpence-worth of chips on the way home. In today's money, that means a special treat night out for twelve and a half pence! Hard to imagine that these days, isn't it?

Then, when I reached the appropriate age, I was allowed to be part of another pastime in the village: I could go on the bus to Carmarthen on a Saturday night. That's the only time I'd go into the town, even though it was no more than a few miles from Bancyfelin. I would be given a pound or two to spend and that would disappear that night, leaving me with no money then for the rest of the week. That bus was jam-packed every Saturday night, with people my age from St Clears, Laugharne, Pendine, and all points in between, heading for a night out in town. By the time the bus reached Bancyfelin, there was hardly any room to sit down. And once in town, we'd go from pub to pub, but we'd always have to make sure that we caught the last bus home at eleven o'clock. I missed that bus many times and there was only one thing to do then, walk the five miles back home. When I did catch the bus, you'd see everyone hanging off it from every possible vantage point, just as we see in TV pictures from places like India these days. Such journeys had their own excitement, an enjoyment I'm sure that young people don't get today when they've all got their own cars or depend on taxis to take them home in the early hours. Saturday night in Carmarthen was a big night out! That's when two kinds of people came together in one place: Carmarthen people were the 'townies' and they called us country folk the 'hambones' or 'boskins'. But we always enjoyed each other's company on Saturday nights.

Another trip we'd have in those days was the chapel's Sunday school trip. We'd go to either Tenby or New Quay, with more than one bus full of people of all ages. It was referred to as the 'big day out' by all. Mothers would prepare a cartload of sandwiches for us to eat on the beach. I've been on very many trips since then, with various teams, all over the world. I don't want to suggest that the Sunday school trips were better than my rugby ones, but they did offer something different, something that's not easy to explain. These chapel trips were the reward for attending Sunday school every week. And Sunday school was part of growing up, an obligation that no-one questioned. Maybe we didn't always want to go to Sunday school, but no-one complained. Now, I look back on those Sunday school days as being a solid foundation for the rest of my life. And it was to those values I returned when my foundations were rocked by my breakdown.

My mother and grandmother spent most of their time in the chapel in the village, but my grandfather spent most of his time in the Fox and Hounds pub. Those two buildings were strong influences in the village, and on my early years. And whatever the individual influences on my life, there's one common theme to the ones I've shared up until now: they were all local. This also meant that everyone else had the same influences, were in the same boat. No-one was different, no-one was an exception. Money meant very little to any of us. Nobody ever felt that they had to go without or were missing out.

When I finished primary school, we moved as a family out of my grandparents' world and into a council house on a new estate on the edge of the village. This was our first home on our own, my mam, my stepfather and the children. My mother had remarried by then. I got on very well with my stepfather, thankfully. He was an electrician from St Clears, which is rather ironic considering that I was brought up in a village that didn't have any electricity! He was a bit of an athlete too, who ran in local competitions. It was a very happy time for us as a family, both in my grandparents' cottage and after we moved to the council house.

In order to get some extra money, my mother took a job delivering the Bancyfelin post. She'd get up at half past six in the morning, so my grandmother had to come up to our house to make sure we all got off to school on time. However, after we moved, I still kept on going back to my grandparents' home regularly, along with my brothers, sisters, and their wives and husbands later. My grandmother would make food for us all and we'd enjoy each other's company. When we all went our separate ways and left the village, I remember my grandmother saying that there was nothing worse than loneliness.

It's from this council house that I went to St Clears Secondary School, where I was able to develop my main sporting interest at that time, football. Rugby wasn't a part of my life, or the life of any other boy in the village, come to that. We played football in primary school and we played football on the streets. Our conversations weren't about rugby, either. We wouldn't talk about Llanelli or Wales rugby stars. Our heroes were Mel Charles, Ivor Allchurch and, of course, Il Gigante Buono himself, John Charles, who played for Leeds and Juventus throughout the 1950s and won 38 caps playing football for Wales. We'd go to watch the Swans playing football at the Vetch, Swansea, now and again, passing Stradey Park on our way. Every village for miles around Bancyfelin had a football team and every summer we'd compete against each other for the Summer Cup. That competition was a highlight for small village football teams throughout the county.

In 1958 the football World Cup was held in Sweden and Wales took part in it for the first time ever. So that cemented the place of football in our lives then. Our small country was in the World Cup finals!

We were aware of rugby, of course. It was mentioned by some local men; we read about it in the papers now and again. Some of us had family members who had played the game to a fairly high level. That was true in my case, too. My mother's brother, Glyn, was capped for the Welsh Schoolboys, as a hooker. I was aware of that, but it didn't affect my early life in any way. Up until about the mid-1950s, rugby was just a visitor in our village, not a resident.

I still enjoy my football and follow the fortunes of the Swans avidly. When there's an opportunity to visit my wife's sister in Manchester, I'll go to watch United or City play. But, of course, rugby *did* come into my life in a big way. But I had to go to the big school for that to happen.

3
Linesman

ON MY FIRST day at St Clears Secondary School there wasn't a rugby post in sight on the school playing fields. But there were goalposts everywhere. That, of course, wasn't a problem for me, no more than it was for the vast majority of other boys in the school. I was chomping at the bit to play football on these fields with my old friends and new classmates. It was a bit of a shock for us all then, when, some time after I started at the school, we saw a set of goalposts being replaced by rugby posts. We couldn't understand at all what was the point of putting them up. No-one played rugby. However, the reason soon became apparent. The school had appointed a new PE teacher and he played rugby for Llanelli RFC. So there was, quite simply, no way that he'd allow only football to be played at the school. Therefore, Howard Davies changed things at the school; he put an end to the football-only tradition. Known as Howard Ash Davies, he was an extremely good prop, who went on to captain the Llanelli side, too.

I wasn't the first boy in our family to start playing

rugby. My two brothers were also at the school. My elder brother, Eddie, was a footballer and a really good cricketer, and he was the one who started to play rugby first. And I have to admit here that he was the best player of the two of us when we were at school. He was bigger than me for a start, and he made quite an impact when he started to play. He was also faster than me, having more presence on the rugby pitch. He played in the second row and sometimes at number 8. We were never to find out how good a player he might have been, because he had to stop playing due to ill health. He sustained an injury when he was about 18 years old and not long afterwards he had to have surgery on his kidneys. He was told by the doctors to stop playing rugby completely.

The introduction of rugby in the school was given a further boost in 1956. That year one of the boys from Bancyfelin was chosen to play for Wales. C.L. Davies was a left wing who played for Cardiff Rugby Club. He got his first cap for a Wales team led by the legendary Cliff Morgan – but that didn't mean much to me at the time! C.L. was a student at University College of Wales, Cardiff, and had started playing rugby after leaving the village. That was a familiar route in those days. People would leave their home villages to go to some college or other and come across the game of rugby while they were studying there.

C.L. was known as Cowboy Davies, although I'm not too sure why. There was great excitement in the village on the day he earned his first cap. There wasn't much hope of anyone from Bancyfelin being able to afford to go to Cardiff to see the match – and we'd have taken all day to get there, anyway! Hardly anyone in the village had a television, but somehow, my mam and stepfather had one in our house. We were, as a result, a very popular family that day! About 20 people squashed into our living room to see the game. Imagine our excitement when C.L. crossed the line for a try, one made even more pleasing because it was in a match against England. There's no doubt that knowing that someone from our village had played for Wales made quite an impression on us young boys. As soon as the game was over we ran like fools through the streets to play rugby against each other.

I started to play rugby for the school team and, not long after that, football was no longer a part of our sporting choices at school at all. We all had to play rugby. The game had taken root properly in the school. Howard Ash started a youth team in St Clears for boys who had left school at 15 years of age. By the end of the 1950s, I'm sure there were about 25 of us in the St Clears Youth Club. From that team, I was chosen to play for Wales Schoolboys.

Howard Ash's influence was, therefore, considerable. He changed the school's sporting tradition completely. He changed me from being an aspiring football player to a rugby player chosen to play for Wales Schools. His contribution was immense, inside and outside the school gates.

When he left the school to take up another teaching position, the youth team didn't survive. It's strange how the influence of just one teacher in a school can be so strong.

Leading the youth team, Howard would keep an eye on the way players developed as they grew older. This became particularly relevant to me as the 1960s started. The Llanelli second row position at that time was held by the legendary R.H. Williams, one of Welsh rugby's biggest stars. He'd started to play for Llanelli as a 19 year old in the 1949/50 season, and captained the club in 1957/58. He'd made an impression on the world rugby stage when he toured with the Lions. On his first tour, to South Africa in 1955, they won 19 games out of 25, with the Test series drawn at two games apiece. On the tour to New Zealand in 1959, he shone during the last Test, winning six line-outs in a row at the end of the game to stop the All Blacks from winning. The Lions ran out winners by 9–6. By the beginning of the 1960 season, however, he'd retired from rugby to concentrate on his job as the Assistant Director of Education in Glamorgan. Llanelli, therefore, needed a new second row. I'd just turned 18 and, as a result, had to stop playing for the youth team. I thought that the path I should take now was to play for either Carmarthen Quins or Carmarthen Athletic. I was trying to make that decision when I saw Howard in St Clears and he told me:

'Llanelli's pre-season trials are coming up soon and I want you to be part of them.'

That was his simple message. My reply was equally simple:

'I really don't think I need to do that. I'm going to either the Quins or the Athletic next.'

Apparently, there had been some speculation about me playing for Llanelli before that conversation, as one or two told me, in no uncertain terms, that it was too soon for me to join Llanelli and that the opportunity would come up again when I was older. That had certainly given me more confidence when telling Howard that I was heading for Carmarthen, not Llanelli. But Howard was ready for my answer and he replied:

'I've put your name down already.'

That was it. Done. When the time came, he took me down to Llanelli himself for the trial. Remember, in those days, there was no such thing as a training coach. The team captain was the man in charge on the field. At Llanelli, that man was Brian Thomas, one of the three second-row players with the club at that time. Howard Jones and John Brock were the other two. John, however, had broken his leg, so they were another second row short. My trial went very well and the captain confirmed that I was in the Llanelli squad. Everything happened so quickly to be honest. I hadn't even been playing the game for that long! But that's what happened, and in the new decade I became a member of the Llanelli Scarlets squad.

I didn't play in the first game of the season but my chance came in the second match. We were playing against a Gerwyn Williams XV. Those kind of fixtures occurred regularly in those days, games against representative teams under various names. Fifteen players from different clubs were chosen to play in the name of an individual or an organisation. The most well-known representative teams, I guess, are the Barbarians and Crawshays.

Gerwyn Williams was a man from Glyncorrwg who used to play full back for Llanelli. He was a member of the Wales Grand Slam-winning team in 1952 and the full back on the day when Wales beat the All Blacks in 1953. After retiring from rugby he taught at many schools in England, and playing against a team of his choice was a regular feature of the Llanelli fixture list for years.

I played in the following game too, against the Irish Wolfhounds. That game was on Monday, 12 September 1960, and the kick-off was at quarter past six. I remember those details because that was the day of my 18th birthday. On the same day, in the village of Mynyddygarreg, a few miles away, a little boy, Ray Gravell, was celebrating his ninth birthday. We hadn't met on that day, of course, but the two of us would go on to share a long rugby career with Llanelli and Wales by the beginning of the 1970s.

On the wing for the Irish Wolfhounds was Sir Anthony Joseph Francis O'Reilly, as he is known today. We knew him as Tony O'Reilly. He was a superb winger who I'd most definitely heard of before facing him on the pitch that day. Knowing he was playing did make me much more nervous. He went on to become Ireland's first billionaire, so they say, having become a successful businessman after hanging up his boots. He established the *Irish Independent* group of newspapers and he has been Chairman of the Heinz group. He most certainly didn't make his money from rugby!

Llanelli had many top-class players in the early 1960s: Aubrey Gale and Marlston Morgan to name but two. Marlston has the amazing, unsurpassable record of playing 465 games for Llanelli, playing the full 80 minutes in every single one! Unbelievable! He captained Llanelli when they played the All Blacks in 1963. The centre that day was D. Ken Jones, one of the Gwendraeth Grammar School boys. He won 14 caps for Wales and six caps for the Lions on two tours, scoring three tries for the Lions as well. Brian Davies was his partner at centre. I was settling into a very talented team, therefore, who would help me develop my own game in a big way. Some people still thought that I was too young to play for Llanelli and some thought that I was too small, as well. Usually, a forward such as myself doesn't reach his prime until he's in his mid-20s. I was only 15 stone, too. There wasn't much I could do about my age, but I did try to do something about my weight. I joined the YMCA in Carmarthen. Every week I'd go there to lift weights. I wouldn't do anything else, like circuit training or whatever, weights were my focus. At that time there was no system at any rugby club to develop players' fitness. You would turn up fit to play and playing made you fitter. Our training sessions were more to do with moves on the pitch, passing, kicking, scrummaging, and so on. Nothing more than that. There was nowhere to do any form of indoor work, there was no gym or anything like that. So we were outside on the pitch at Stradey in sun, rain and snow. More often than not it was a case of finishing work on the two training nights each week and going straight over to Stradey. If there was time to go home, it would only be long enough to have a cup of tea.

I worked for the Electricity Board at that time. I started to work for them the same year I started playing for Llanelli. I was a linesman, which meant spending a lot of time climbing electricity poles in all weathers to ensure that everyone had their electricity supply. It was interesting work as I met a variety of people. The work was particularly challenging during the heavy snow of 1963. That year, as in 1947, the snow lay deep on the ground for about two months. We had to walk through the snow to get to damaged or broken electricity lines. These were, of course, the days before the common use of JCBs!

There's no doubt that the nature of my job contributed to my general fitness. It gave me some sort of natural strength that can't be developed in gyms. I still did the weights of course, and they were important. But the physical work I did every day was a significant contribution to my fitness. As the years went by, and I played more and more for Llanelli, people at work got to know what I did in my spare time, and that was always a great excuse to have long chats about rugby. But it did also have its downside. If anything went wrong on a job, there was no place for me to hide. A message would go back to the office saying that such and such wasn't working properly and they would add 'the footballer was here doing the job'! In time another player did exactly the same work as me in the Llanelli area, Ray Gravell.

I worked in the Carmarthen area, but different areas were soon united and I had to work as far afield as the Lampeter and Cardigan areas. It was quite common for me to travel up past Llan-non, Cardiganshire, and up towards Aberystwyth, or down to Mynachlog-ddu and Crymych, or across the Tywi Valley to Llandovery. Working in such a large area meant visiting hundreds of farms and I was very happy doing that. In the early days, the farms were owned by Welsh country people and were part of the agricultural heritage of Wales. But I did see a definite change as the years went by, with the number of people moving in from outside the area increasing significantly. Normally that didn't cause any problems for me in my work, but sometimes it did. I remember one story in the Llandovery area. There had been bad storms one year and many farms lost their electricity supply completely. We then had to work our way from house to house, working out where the supply had been broken and then restoring it. I'd been doing this for two whole days, without going home. It was a large area, with farms spread over great distances. I arrived at one farmhouse, feeling shattered from the work I'd done up until then. The farmer came to meet me:

'I know your bloody game!' he said very abruptly, 'Just because I'm English, you've deliberately left me till last!'

Nothing was further from the truth, by the way. But that's how he saw things. Having to deal with attitudes like that was a new experience for me in my work and I wasn't used to it.

Back at Stradey, my work and visits to the YMCA had borne fruit. I'd gone up to 16 stone, ten pounds, in a fairly short space of time. With some luck, I've managed to keep at about that same weight throughout my life. I might actually be a little bit lighter now than when I was playing. The weight gain gave me an extra advantage in my game. Howard Ash had told me early on that I'd be good in the line-out because I had a natural spring that meant I could reach greater heights to get the ball. I had to make sure that I could still keep that spring despite putting on weight. Dealing with injuries was also a different matter then. There were no substitutes. So, it was simple: if you had an injury you had to either carry on playing with it or leave the field, but that left your team a man short for the remainder of the game. I can remember many a match when there were quite a few players hobbling around the field waiting desperately for that final whistle!

Whatever the weather, however tough your working day or training session had been, there was always one thing to look forward to eagerly on training nights. The bag man at Llanelli in those days was a character called Tiss. He took it his responsibility to make sure that we all had something tidy to eat at the end of the night. Twice a week, as we trudged off the Stradey pitch, we'd walk into the dressing room where platefuls of sandwiches and a jar of pickles were laid on for us. They were most welcome! There were no showers, of course, so we'd all bath together in one massive tub. You had to make sure that you got into the bath early enough, or you'd be jumping into water that was already filthy from all the other players (and you could possibly come out dirtier than when you went in!). But there's no doubt that this camaraderie was a central part of being in a rugby team and a big part of the fun, too!

The Stradey stadium in those days was very basic. The South Stand had been built and there was some form of shelter at the Pwll End. The famous Tanner Bank was a mound of rubble, which was assembled – it would be too formal to say 'built' – from bricks and stone from various local Second World War shelters. The Tanner Bank was where all the characters would stand to watch games. And that's where the more witty or colourful comments would come from! As the pitch was so close to the spectators there, we'd have no problem hearing every comment, however quiet! At the Eastern End, throughout most of the 1960s, there was no scoreboard. But by 1972, the scoreboard placed at the Eastern End would go on to become famous, showing as it did the Llanelli/All Blacks 9–3 score. But in the 1960s it was only a mound of rubble.

The town was very different, too. Between Stradey and the sea, the massive Llanelli steelworks stood imposingly, a huge black and grey structure that spread for quite some distance along the main road out of town. It was called the Klondike by the townspeople, because of the wealth perceived to come into the town when it first opened at the end of the 19th century. Very many Llanelli players worked at the Klondike, and, of course, many more fans worked there. In the 1960s Llanelli was still a town of heavy industries, as it was in the days when the club was first formed. Any new factory opening was likely to be in the car components' industry. The toil of the working week was inextricably linked to the Saturday afternoon rugby game. The sweat and graft was eased and rewarded by those few hours spent watching the game and enjoying a pint with your co-workers and fellow fans. It was a ritual. Many would go straight from their Saturday morning shift to the game. Many players did that, too.

In my first season at Llanelli I had another new experience – flying! Well, what a shock! I hadn't travelled far from home, yet alone *flown* anywhere. Even going to London was a big shock to the system. Llanelli had a fixture against the Dublin Wanderers at their home. So we needed to catch a plane from Cardiff to get there. It was all new to me.

The next new experience came in 1963 when

Llanelli were to play the mighty All Blacks. Nobody needed to tell us about their ability and talent. I'd heard enough about them from Howard Ash in school. As is the case when inquisitive schoolboys come across something new, I had to find out more about these players our teacher was talking about. So I turned to the newspapers regularly from then on to look for All Blacks stories. As a result, realising that these very men would be coming to play at my home ground was overwhelming. I knew that the Stradey pitch would be quivering under the feet of people such as Wilson Whineray, Brian Lochore, Waka Nathan, Don Clarke, Colin Meads, and others.

The preparation for the game was in the hands of our captain, Marlston Morgan, and the routine was no different from that of any other training week. When the selections were announced, I was in the team but, not only that, I'd also be marking the legendary Colin Meads, then a 21 year old in the early years of his career. There were no means of studying your opponents' play, no videos or anything like that at the time. We had to rely on reading reports about them in newspapers.

When the game got underway on 31 December 1963, we were ahead at half-time and had given them a tough game. But they decided to turn the screw in the second half, and eventually went on to win by 16 points to eight. I learned a lesson that day, watching the way the All Blacks approached and played the game. They were hard, tough boys, with not an ounce of waste fat on their bodies, especially Colin Meads, or Pinetree as he was called. However, he hadn't been anywhere near a gym in his life. He'd built his strength working on his farm back home, like so many of the other players, too. That said, one of our boys left his mark on one of Meads' team-mates that day. Terry Price was our full back and only 18 years of age. But he managed to break the jaw of no less an opponent than Waka Nathan, the one they called the Black Panther. That says it all. Waka had to return home after the game, thanks to Terry. If anyone asks me today who is the best full back I've seen play, I still say Terry Price. I'd choose him before JPR and all the other great full backs.

After the game, the official dinner was held at Stradey itself. I don't think there was a hotel in Llanelli that could have held such a dinner in those days. The highlight of that function for me was being able to exchange ties with Colin Meads. I felt very special being able to do so. I certainly wasn't shy in showing that tie to everybody afterwards – surely things couldn't get much better than that!

I learned that there was a different way of playing rugby that day, a way centred on the forwards. There wasn't a better group of forwards that I could learn from than that All Blacks front eight who were at Stradey in 1963. At that time, throughout my career, and up until the present day, I've not seen a better pack of forwards on a rugby field than the New Zealand forwards who played between 1963 and 1967. They were unbelievable.

I followed avidly all the newspaper match reports for the rest of their games on that tour. They only lost one, that famous game at Newport. I was an established player in the Llanelli squad. The first two years were quite difficult ones, I must say. It wasn't easy going from St Clears Youth to a team like Llanelli, and I found it difficult to settle into the game. I was playing against people who'd been playing first-class rugby for years. They'd represented their country and the Lions. Yes, I had a lot to learn – about rugby, and about life as well. I managed to survive and Howard Ash deserves a great deal of credit for that. There was no way in the world that I'd have considered joining Llanelli of my own accord. I might have thought about trying to join them when I was about 25, maybe. But, by the time I did reach that age I'd been on a tour with the British and Irish Lions. Thank goodness, there are people in this world who have superior vision than one's self sometimes.

4

Spandau

AFTER A FEW seasons playing for Llanelli, the chance
came to try to win my place in the Wales team. In
those days, the national team was chosen following
a game between two teams, the Probables (red)
and the Possibles (white). The first-choice Wales
internationals played in red and those knocking on
the door for selection played in white. There were
exceptions, of course, but this was usually the pattern
of things. The Wales second row at the time consisted
of Roddy Evans, Brian Price, Brian Thomas and Ian
Ford. They were big, strong players, and a lot older
than me. I was happy enough to be chosen to play for
the Possibles, so that I could start to understand the
game at international level. I was up against Brian
Price in my first trial, in 1965, and all I can say is
that I had another lesson that day, too! Suffice to add
that I wasn't chosen for the Wales team.

At about the same time I had an opportunity to
go abroad with Llanelli. The club had arranged a
tour in Germany. We sailed over to Ostend, then
travelled through Belgium and into Germany, or
West Germany as it was called then, of course. The

Second World War had come to an end 20 years previously but there were still sensitivities about that. We had to go through checkpoints every now and then and, when that happened, German soldiers would come aboard the bus to search our belongings. Every single one of us, tough rugby players or not, sat in fear when this happened, not saying a word as the soldiers searched. The bus also had to be driven over a huge mirror so that the underside of the vehicle could be examined. There may well have been two decades since the end of hostilities, but it didn't appear as if things were much friendlier.

We played games in Mönchengladbach, a city lying between Düsseldorf and the border with the Netherlands. This city was the home of the famous Borussia Mönchengladbach football team. That year, they'd just won promotion for the first time to the Bundesliga, the top German league which had only formed two years prior to that in 1963. Bayern Munich also entered the Bundesliga for the first time that year, too. So, when we got there, it was no surprise to see football generating such excitement in the city. But there was enough interest in rugby too, to make a tour by a team from west Wales worthwhile.

We also went to Berlin. That's where all that we'd read or heard about the Second World War came alive right in front of our eyes. The Berlin Wall had been built only four years prior to our tour. The reason for building it, of course, depends on which side of the wall you're standing. For those whom we were visiting on the western side of the wall, it was built to stop people fleeing from the Communist east of the city to the West. Seeing all those soldiers along the wall, the miles of threatening barbed wire, and Checkpoint Charlie, was enough to fill you with fear. It was very intimidating, to be honest. I'm sure that was because the wall hadn't been up for very long, and tensions were still quite fresh.

We were staying in one of the military camps of the British Armed Forces. The British Army had been responsible for introducing rugby to the country in the first place, along with a few German public schools. We were staying and playing in the Spandau area of Berlin, in a camp that was home to the prison of the same name. Following the 1947 Nuremberg Trials, seven prisoners were detained at this camp for their part in Nazi atrocities. Of the seven, the most infamous was Rudolph Hess. He, along with two of the others, was still imprisoned when we played rugby there. At that time he was refusing to see anyone and didn't agree to see his son and daughter until 1969. He died at the prison in 1987, having been an inmate for 40 years. I wonder to myself, now and again, whether Hess peeped out of his cell window to watch us play rugby that day!

The Second World War halted the development of rugby in Germany. Before the fighting, France and Germany were the two prominent rugby nations on mainland Europe, with Germany securing top spot a year before the war. But many of their players were killed between 1939 and 1945, and although rugby hasn't disappeared completely from the country, they now play in the third tier of world rugby and have never succeeded in reaching the rugby world cup finals. Despite that, there are about a hundred clubs in Germany today, so they tell me. I hope the game prospers once again in that now unified country.

It was a strange experience going on that tour. Prior to that, we only knew of one conversation that involved the Germans, or 'Jyrmans' as we'd call them back home. That would be talking about the war, destruction and killing they'd inflicted on us. That was particularly pertinent in west Wales because of what the Luftwaffe did to Swansea in the Blitz of 1941, less than a year before I was born. Swansea aflame was the topic of conversation for a long time. I didn't understand much of it when I was a child, but I grew to understand it.

And there we were – in the country of these people, playing rugby. I don't know to this day what was behind the decision of the Llanelli committee to arrange a tour of West Germany. Not that much earlier, Llanelli RFC had been on a tour to Moscow in 1957, even closer to the war period and the time of leaders such as Stalin in that country. I remember Howard Ash mentioning the tour to us boys at St Clears Secondary School. He'd been, so had a certain Carwyn James. Tours to Germany and Russia were very rare in those sensitive Cold War days, but Llanelli visited both within a decade.

I'm sure that this was an indication of two things. Firstly, the colour of politics in our corner of Wales, and also a strong sense that rugby could rise above politics when push came to shove. This last point came to the surface a few years later when the whole issue of apartheid in South Africa reared its ugly head. That tour of Germany for me was about much more than just rugby. Much of what I'd learned in school came back to me in a real way on that trip. I'm sure that every player on that German tour asked themselves at some point, 'What on the earth am I doing here?' Up until that point, the Jyrmans were one thing and one thing only, the enemy. But, out there, we had to differentiate between rugby and history. We had to accept that we were out there to play rugby at a time when hostilities had officially ceased.

5

Budgies

LESS THAN A year later, I was at Paddington station, sitting alongside my fellow Llanelli player and friend, Marlston Morgan, under the massive clock that hung from the iron girders. Our train back to west Wales was running half an hour late. Yes, such things even happened in the good old days of steam! Llanelli had just played against one of the London teams the day before, I think it was Wasps. We'd all travelled to London on the Friday, played on Saturday and were to travel back on the Sunday. Maybe the game was only 80 minutes, as now, but we needed a good three days away from home in order to play in London. On that Sunday afternoon, we were all anxious to get back home. Marlston and I sat there glancing up at the clock every other minute to see how long we had to wait for our train home. We watched every move of the hands on the clock until we heard the puffing of the train in the distance. Having been away from home for a while, a half-hour's delay seemed like ages to us.

The train arrived at the platform at last and I was now heading back home to Carmarthen. From there

I'd get a lift back to Bancyfelin. I was dropped off in the village and walked up to our house on the council estate. As I approached, I noticed a group of about a dozen people standing outside my home. I got a little anxious on seeing them, and wondered what was wrong. As I got closer, I noticed that there were two photographers there as well. That confused me even more. Why on the earth were they there? In the middle of the crowd, I saw my stepfather rushing about like a madman.

'You're going on the Lions tour! You're going with the Lions! You're going to New Zealand!'

He was very excitable, as was everybody else there. I was just dazed. There was a lot of hand clapping, back-slapping, shouting and cheering, and slowly the story emerged. My mam had received a phone call to say that I'd indeed been selected for the Lions tour of New Zealand. I hadn't even played for Wales at that point, so being chosen for the Lions was even more of shock! I often think, as Marlston and I were sitting under that clock at Paddington, that everybody in Bancyfelin was waiting for me – to share the news! The whole village knew a long time before I did!

Our house was complete chaos from then on. Everyone was so jubilant, and unable to hide it even if they wanted to! The whole scenario was so new to everyone and it meant so much to a small village like Bancyfelin that one from its midst had been chosen to play for the Lions. I, on the other hand, didn't have much space or time to think about what it all meant to me. The only thing I was clear about was that thoughts of going on a Lions tour hadn't even entered my head in the preceding weeks and months. The reason was obvious: I hadn't played for Wales, so playing for the Lions was impossible. I'd played a few games for the Possibles, but hadn't reached the Probables, as two exceptional players, giants of 1960s rugby, were keeping me out of the Wales team, Brian Price and Brian Thomas.

Because I'd played for the Possibles, I did receive a formal letter from the organisers of the Lions tour which asked me were I chosen, would I be available to go? I took that as a circular letter, sent out to dozens of British and Irish players, and not significant in any way. However, the letter had to be answered. I replied, but without checking with my employers if I'd be allowed to go, as I didn't think it was a serious show of interest.

It was like a fair outside and inside our home in Bancyfelin for hours after I returned from London. I don't know what it was like at the Fox and Hounds pub down the road! John Scone, a man from the village, kept the pub in those days. Singing was an essential part of pub life for him. When the time was right, he'd jump on a chair and start the singing himself, with everyone else joining in. If the singing wasn't good enough for him, he'd stop and tell them to start again: 'Hold it boys! You can do better than that, shape it!'

That Sunday afternoon, however, there was no need to encourage anyone to sing or improve their singing. And, of course, it being a Sunday, the pubs weren't supposed to be open anyway. But not only was the Fox open, it didn't close until breakfast time the following day, with half the village not managing to go to work on that Monday morning! What an occasion!

The buzz remained in the village for days. At some point, possibly later on that Sunday, I started to think what the whole thing meant to me personally. It wasn't easy to accept what had just happened. Being chosen for the Lions started to frighten me a little. I'd hardly been away from home throughout my life, only a handful of away games with Llanelli and the trip to Germany. North Wales was like a foreign country to me! I'm a man of my square mile and I was even more so in those days. Going with the Lions meant a trip to the other side of the world and being away from home for five long months. So, alongside the pride of being selected in the first place, there were many fears and doubts.

Something else was pressing on me too and causing me some worry about being away for so long. Throughout my schooldays I'd kept budgies. I probably had about 50 of them at the time I heard about the Lions tour. What would happen to them when I was away for so long? It was even more worrying because I'd be away over the summer – the budgies' breeding time.

Another concern was the fact that I'd hardly know anyone on the tour. The main reason for that being the fact that I hadn't played for Wales and, therefore, the international players and the whole set-up was foreign to me. I did know many of the Wales internationals through the club scene, of course. That was my main comfort. I lost a lot of sleep worrying about all these things I must say, worrying about how I was going to cope on such a level.

Nevertheless, what carried me through was the way the Bancyfelin people reacted and responded to the news. I'd also played enough rugby to realise how much of an honour this was and that carried me forward as well. I started to accept the situation therefore, and being selected began to sit a lot more comfortably with me.

But there was one problem left. I still had to ask my employer if I could have the time off to go on the tour. How was I going to deal with that little request? It was quite some thing to ask for five months off work! It just didn't happen in my experience, but I had to ask.

I went in to work on the Monday and to Mr Lefèvre's office to explain what had happened the day before, and to request the time off. His reaction was simple: 'Congratulations! You've been chosen to go, leave it to me, you will be going!'

A week later, he came back to me and confirmed that I'd definitely be going and, more than that, I'd be going on full pay as well! Amazing! When I did eventually join the Lions squad I soon learned that about half of them had to go without pay for the duration of the tour. Alun Pask, for example, was a teacher, as was Brian Price. They weren't paid a halfpenny for the whole five months with the Lions.

That was a huge sacrifice for them and their families in order to have the honour of wearing a Lions jersey. As far as I was concerned, the Electricity Board couldn't have been more supportive. And I repaid the favour as, by the time I retired, I'd worked for them for 47 years.

But, if my employer was special in its support, so too were the Bancyfelin villagers who helped me and my family prepare for my time in the southern hemisphere. I had all sorts of support from them, with everyone wanting to make sure that I was OK, that I wanted for nothing, and that my family was all right, too. They continued to look after my family in small, practical ways throughout the time I was away. No wonder that Bancyfelin has such a warm place in my heart to this day. That's where my roots are, even though I've lived in Carmarthen for over 30 years. And, when I did leave to go on tour, my brother, thankfully, looked after my budgies the best he could!

6
Lions

I MET OTHER members of that Lions squad for the first time in Eastbourne. The manager, Des O'Brien from Ireland, had called us all down there for a week in mid-April so that we could start our training. Those mixed feelings about being chosen for the Lions returned to the front of my mind that week. It's hard to imagine how a country boy like me could walk into a posh hotel to meet over 30 of the best players in Britain and Ireland, and then begin to try to make sense of it all. I'm not too clever in mixing with people at the best of times and I don't usually have much to say to strangers. This, in addition to the fact that I'd be so far away from home once the tour got underway properly.

By the time I arrived in Eastbourne there were other things going through my mind as well. On the one hand, it was a massive help that there were so many Welsh players in the squad. Eleven of the 32-strong squad were Welsh. That's a higher proportion, if not a higher number, than the Welsh boys in the Lions squad in Australia in 2013 – and a lot of fuss was made about that. We had Dewi Bebb, Ken Jones,

Stuart Watkins, Allan Lewis and David Watkins in the backs, and Denzil Williams, Brian Price, Alun Pask, Howard Norris and Gareth Prothero in the forwards, and myself of course. I'd played with David Watkins, Newport's talented outside-half and Allan Lewis, Abertillery's scrum half, in the Wales Youth team. The others were regular opponents, week in, week out, on Welsh rugby fields. In addition, the trainer was Welshman John Robins. He was the first man given the title 'coach' on a Lions tour. Prior to that, the manager and deputy manager would take full responsibility for everything on tour, on and off the field. John Robins was a prop in his playing days and he played for Wales eleven times at the start of the 1950s. He didn't play for any Welsh club however, playing his club rugby in England for teams such as Coventry, Sale and Leicester. He also had the unusual distinction of winning two caps for England during the Second World War. He played for the England Military Services team and saw active service with the Navy.

I would, therefore, be surrounded by plenty of fellow Welshmen. But something made me stand out from the other players at that Eastbourne hotel: I hadn't been capped by my country. That made me different. It meant I didn't fit in. I didn't understand the same things as the others and I felt out of my depth. But, that week in Eastbourne went some way to easing those fears and I proved the benefit of being there by the time we left. The next journey with the squad would be much further and longer.

I've no idea if the management noticed my nervousness while I was in Eastbourne, but they couldn't have chosen a better room-mate for me on the first leg of the tour in Australia. I was to room with Scotsman Jim Telfer. He was the Scottish number 8 in the 1960s and went on to coach the Lions tour of New Zealand in 1983. Jim made his mark on rugby folklore during a speech he gave as assistant manager of the 1997 tour to South Africa. He was primarily responsible for the forwards on that tour and, before the first Test, he took the forwards to one side and shared with them some of the Lions rugby heritage. Faced with the finest forwards in Britain and Ireland, he said, 'This is your Everest boys. Very few get the chance to go to the top of Everest. You have the chance today…' He went on to say that many are *considered* to wear that jersey but only a few are *chosen*. That reference to Everest has entered the lexicon of rugby sayings. Jim himself parodied his own speech in 2013 when he addressed a group of Lions supporters out in Australia.

But, of course, all that was in front of Jim when he shared his room with a boy from Bancyfelin in Sydney in 1966. What followed showed what kind of man he was. I can't specify exactly what his main contribution to helping me settle was. I don't know if it was the influence of his rugby ability, his latent coaching skills, or the fact that he obviously had man management talents as headmaster of Hawick High School. Whatever it was, he helped me settle and made me feel a part of the team. Jim and I became good friends after that.

Another Welshman joined us out there, the genius Terry Price. The first-choice full back, Don Rutherford from England, had broken his arm and Terry was called upon to replace him. It was good news for the Lions when a player of his obvious ability was called out, and it was good news for me too, as he was a fellow Welsh-speaking Llanelli team-mate whom I knew well. He hadn't been chosen for the tour originally because of a knee injury. That had improved by the time he joined the rest of us, but not anywhere good enough to cope with a tour at that level. He only played about two games in the end, and I'm sure that under today's conditions, he wouldn't have played at all.

We changed room-mates every time we changed hotels. Thank goodness I started with Jim Telfer, because the next man I shared a room with was the colourful Irishman, Willie John McBride. If the word 'character' was ascribed for anyone, it was for Willie John. He was, and is, a giant, mischievous Irishman, always up to some trick or other, morning, noon and night. When he realised that I was to share with him, he turned to me and said: 'Don't worry Del, you follow me, you won't go far wrong!'

I often think that if I'd listened to those words and followed him in all that he did, I might not be here today! But, despite that side of him, he was always by my side if I needed him. Quite often, that big hand of his would fall on my shoulder as he uttered words of encouragement on the field. He, too, was a country boy, raised on a farm in Ireland, and we could talk about the same things. Perhaps because we have the same 'country' blood pumping through our veins, we became very good friends and that remains to this day.

After about three weeks on tour, everything seemed to settle down for me, the initial heartache and fear disappeared. When these had been at their worst, I couldn't see a way out, as the tour was to take a long five months. The thought of such a length of time made things a lot worse. Tours aren't that long now, of course: after three weeks, the tour is half over!

I soon realised that the other players wanted me to feel part of the team. It's easy to think, I suppose, that players in a competitive team situation don't want to support each other because they either want your place themselves or they would prefer someone else to have your place. You were never too sure of those playing in the same position as you, for example. One of the second row on that tour was Lions captain, Mike Campbell-Lamerton, which is where Willie John McBride also played. But, such thoughts of niggle and rivalry soon disappeared. For my part, I decided that it was best to keep quiet, quieter than usual for me, to test the waters a little first before diving in. I reminded myself that I'd been chosen to be part of the Lions squad for a reason. I had to hold on to that the best I could when given the opportunity.

One man played a big part in all this process. My

Uncle Vincent, my mother's brother. He'd moved to Australia in 1947 when I was a five-year-old boy. A mechanic, he'd upped sticks to the other side of the world to find a new life. By the time I set foot on Australian soil, he'd been there for nearly 20 years – and he had a house on Bondi Beach! I didn't remember a great deal about him from when he lived in Wales. I do remember him taking me and my brother on a bus to Carmarthen to buy us a pair of Wellington boots! After three weeks in Australia with the Lions, we'd reached Sydney, and I'll never forget seeing him walk into our hotel. It was a lovely feeling and an emotional moment for both of us. I'm sure that he had a bit of a shock seeing how I'd grown up. I spent quite a lot of time with him after that, in the hotel, in his house on the beach, and in Sydney itself. And, even though such close and strong links with back home could have made settling on the tour harder for me, it didn't have that effect, thank goodness. Quite the contrary, it was a big help. It was a different tour from then on.

I realised early on that the Irish players were a special group of people when on tour. They had definite warmth that pulled other people together. That certainly was Willie John's gift, but also people such as Noel Murphy's too; he went on to captain Munster, be Ireland's coach, and Lions coach in 1980.

On the pitch, we played a few games in Australia before flying over to New Zealand for the main leg of the tour. We played eight games in Australia, including two Test matches. I wasn't chosen for either of those, but the second Test is certainly memorable. It was a comfortable victory for the Lions, 31–0, against an Australian team that included the star Ken Catchpole as scrum half. Dewi Bebb and Dai Watkins scored a try each and Ken Jones scored two. A good day for the Welsh! I'd been chosen for the very first game of the tour, against Western Australia in Perth. We won comfortably, 60–3. That was my first taste of rugby at that level and I felt quite proud of myself as I walked off the pitch at the end of the game.

Arriving in New Zealand was quite a shock to the system, I must say. In Australia, we played on hard, firm grounds in baking sun. When we crossed to Invercargill, we were right in the middle of heavy rain and mud! Not that the weather was the only difference. There was also no means of comparing the quality and the nature of the rugby, either. That's where the tour started properly, in New Zealand. In the game against Taranaki, for example, I went up for the ball in a line-out and felt my legs knocked from underneath me. When I landed on the ground, seven or eight All Blacks forwards were on top of me rucking everything but the ball. I broke two ribs in that game. The referee was the only official in those days, no touch judges or any other officials; one man in the middle of 30 others. There was little he could do, really. They weren't neutral referees, either. On that tour, as in all others at that time, the referees were from the host country.

Games were certainly rougher in those days. I

had another injury later on in the tour when I hit the ground like a sack of potatoes in another line-out, but this time I damaged my shoulder. In order to protect my injury a little, I put a piece of foam on my shoulder underneath my jersey. The referee saw it and came up and told me to take it out. His words were quite simple: 'You're either fit to play or you're not! Take it out.'

I had to obey, of course. With an injury there was no way I was going to be selected for the Test matches in New Zealand. Mike Campbell-Lamerton and Brian Price were the first-choice second row, with Willie John and myself as second choice. We took a bit of a beating in the first Test, 20 points to three, I think. That shook us a bit. The management decided that changes were needed for the second Test. As a result, Willie John and I were chosen ahead of the other two second-rowers. That was such a massive shock to me.

Early in that game, I managed to steal the ball in a line-out from their throw. Their prop, Ken Gray, came up to me at the first opportunity and stared me straight in the eyes, quite menacingly, and he put his nose against mine: 'Take another ball like that and I'll take your f*****g head off!'

Welcome to New Zealand rugby! He knew, of course, that I was an inexperienced player. But I was experienced enough to know that I shouldn't pay any attention to what he said. I didn't, and the rest of the game went well. We did lose, but the game could have gone either way right up until the end. When the final whistle blew, I was even prouder of myself than when walking off after my first Lions match in Western Australia. I had just won my first cap for the British and Irish Lions.

As we all sat in the changing room afterwards, the door opened and in came the All Blacks manager, Fred Allen. He came straight across to me and said: 'Put this in your drawer.' In his hand, right in front of me, was an All Blacks shirt. He realised that I hadn't had a cap for my country yet, and he wanted me to have something to remember my first Lions cap. That was such a special gesture and it still means so much to me now, especially when I realised that he'd given me Colin Meads' shirt! He was a giant in the land of giants, one of the all-time greats of New Zealand rugby. It was an honour to have played against him – but I can't say it was a pleasure! It was even more of an honour to be given one of his shirts. I was given his tie after the Llanelli-All Blacks game three years earlier. Now I had a shirt he played in as well.

Before the third Test, I clearly remember going to the hotel room of one of the boys so that we could watch the football World Cup final between England and West Germany. The room was packed full of as many players as could be squeezed in. We were on the other side of the world, but were enjoying the excitement of the game and cheering when Geoff Hurst scored his goals enabling England to win the World Cup.

The biggest thrill for the Welsh Lions on that tour was meeting Welsh people who'd moved to live in the southern hemisphere. Many would come to the hotels where we were staying in order to say hello and have a chat. It had happened in Australia too, but I wasn't in such a position to appreciate it then, apart from my uncle's visit, of course. Many who called to see us in New Zealand enjoyed the rare opportunity to talk about Wales and to do so in Welsh as well, as many of the Welsh players were Welsh speakers. We were invited to their homes for a meal or a coffee; they were very special evenings, with a warm Welsh welcome guaranteed. Home cooking was certainly a welcome relief from hotel food! The links were even stronger if our ex-pat Welsh hosts were from the same area as some of the players; the conversation would flow long into the night if we established mutual acquaintances, friends or relations. In my case, I was particularly happy when an invitation came to visit some of the Welsh who farmed in New Zealand. I was in my element then. I didn't have much love for big places like Auckland or Christchurch, and the other boys soon cottoned on to that. Whenever we'd fly into one of the small towns, on an island maybe, the chorus would rise from behind me somewhere: 'Oh! this is Del country now, boys!'

Such a connection with compatriots abroad didn't seem to flow to such an extent with players from the other nations on the Lions tour. Players from England, Ireland and Scotland were always amazed as to how the Welsh emigrants would come looking for Welsh players to socialise with. That was a big factor for me on the 1966 tour, quite something to behold and experience. I experienced it many times after that too, with the Lions and Wales. It was particularly true in Australia and New Zealand, but not so much perhaps in South Africa. We had a special welcome from native New Zealanders, too. We hardly had to pay for anything; if we wanted to go to the cinema, tickets would be made available for us. New Zealanders are special people and would give you anything – apart from the 80 minutes on the pitch, that is!

As a squad we had a daily allowance to spend: ten shillings a day (50 pence nowadays). Willie John McBride, a bank manager in his day job, was in charge of handing the money out. We had to stand in a line in front of his desk, so that he could give us the money and tick our names off the register. On the side of that register was a column entitled 'Hotel Damages'. If there was a need to pay for any damage caused to the hotel or its property by the players, it would be deducted from the ten shillings. That would apply to everyone, whether you were responsible for the damage or not. It was quite common for damage to be caused by one or two, but the whole lot of us would have our allowance docked! Ironically, it was our very own bank manager who was likelier than most to have caused any damage. But if anyone dared question the fairness of such a system, Willie John would have a short, sharp response: 'We're in this together!'

Back to matters on the field. The captain Mike Campbell-Lamerton was really anxious to get back in the team for the third Test match, and he was selected. Willie John was selected to play alongside him. But, I was also chosen for that game – as a prop! My second Lions Test cap, therefore, was as a tight-head prop so that room could be made for the captain to return to the team. Like any other player, I'm sure, I'd happily play anywhere if it meant getting a game. But, being thrown into the front row in an international, on the tight head, was certainly a very different experience. And, of course, who was I propping against? None other than Ken Gray, the same man who had previously threatened me! I don't think such a situation would arise in an international today. I had a fairly decent game, but I soon realised that there was a lot more to international propping than people thought. I was also chosen to play prop in the fourth and final Test. But I injured my back and the usual prop, Welshman Denzil Williams, was chosen instead.

The tour came to an end, but we hadn't managed to win one Test match in New Zealand. I'd learned what real rugby was like, playing against the All Blacks. The day we left Auckland for Honolulu was also my birthday. We crossed the international time line – so I had another full birthday in Hawaii! That was a year of two September 12s for me, one in Auckland and one in Honolulu.

The Honolulu visit was a stopover on our way to Canada. The organisers obviously thought that we hadn't been away long enough or hadn't played enough rugby! So they added a few extra games in

Canada, 'on our way home'! The first Test in Canada proved to be difficult. Many of our boys found it extremely painful to wear their Lions shirts, due to excess sunbathing in Hawaii! Some were really suffering and we lost that first Test to Canada. Everyone was better by the second Test, which we went on to win. Then it really was time to head back home.

There would be more Lions tours for me in the years to come. One, in particular, would be more memorable in terms of success. But, as I look back on my career, I can say that it's the 1966 tour that has a special place in my heart. I'm sure that might sound strange to many, especially now that one is aware of what happened in 1971. But it's true. The reasons for it are quite clear: that was the first time I had a proper taste of top-level rugby; the first time I'd gone to the other side of the world, so far from home; the first time I'd been chosen to represent anyone at an international level and that for the British and Irish Lions; the first time I'd experienced the might of the All Blacks' way of playing rugby. It was an eye-opener on so many levels.

Back home, my mother and stepfather came to London to meet me off the plane and take me home. That was quite some effort in those days, I must say. Seeing them standing there waiting for me was quite an emotional experience, especially as there hadn't been any contact between us for five months. And, of course, my mother wanted to know everything about her brother. As we approached Bancyfelin, they insisted that I sat on the bonnet of the car, so that they could drive into the village with me in full view. All the villagers came out to welcome me home and they stood either side of the road clapping and cheering. Seeing the faces of some of the older villagers standing in their doorways made quite an impression on me. I saw one of them, Trevor Hughes. We'd chatted just as I left for Eastbourne all those months earlier and, as he placed his hand on my shoulder, he'd said that day, 'Delme, put Bancyfelin on the map!' Seeing him there on my return, and everyone else, made me realise that I'd managed to do just that. The Fox and Hounds, of course, was right at the centre of all the celebrations as it was on the day it was announced that I was selected for the tour. Everyone had followed all the games on the radio or in newspaper reports and they had, therefore, learned that I'd earned two Test caps for the Lions.

The village where you are born is sure to have an enormous influence on you throughout your life. I thought the world of Bancyfelin before 1966. But, since that tour, the village has meant so much more to me because of the way everybody pulled together to support me and my family. I'll never forget that feeling for as long as I live.

A week after I returned home, the world was rocked by the horrific news of what had happened in Aberfan, when 116 children were killed in Pantglas Junior School. Some events put a game of rugby in its proper context.

7

Dragons

WITH MY FEET firmly back on Welsh soil, I was more determined than ever to try to get into the Wales team. The fact that I'd already toured with the Lions would be a major boost to my hopes. I finally got the call to join the Wales set-up not long after coming home from the Lions tour. Ironically, I'd win my first cap against Australia in December 1966.

Two other players also received their first caps in that Australia game: two who would go on to make quite an impression on the game of rugby worldwide, Barry John and Gerald Davies. Gerald wore number 12 on his back in that game and he wouldn't move to the wing for some years. Terry Price also played in that game. The routine in those days was for the Wales squad to meet on a Thursday afternoon at the South Wales Police ground in Bridgend. That's where we'd have our training session and then return home and go to work as usual on the Friday. On Friday night we'd travel to the Angel Hotel in Cardiff for about six o'clock. We wouldn't meet as a squad all that often, that 'system' hadn't started yet.

We lost against Australia, 11–14, but it was a very

close game. That was the only occasion Wales played Australia at home throughout the 1960s (Wales travelled to Australia three years later). Australia had last visited in 1958, and their next tour wouldn't be until 1973. How different from the situation today when we see all the southern hemisphere countries here nearly every year now.

The team in which I played my first game for Wales included: Terry Price, Stuart Watkins, John Dawes, Gerald Davies, Dewi Bebb, Barry John and Allan Lewis at the back, with forwards Denzil Williams, Norman Gale, John Lloyd, Brian Price, me, Ken Braddock, Haydn Morgan, and Alun Pask as captain. That's quite a team, I must say, with many stars in their midst – some who were stars at the time and others who would become great stars.

On that same tour, as happened each time a foreign team came to these shores, the visitors would play a team consisting of players from several clubs. In 1966 Australia played against a XV chosen from Neath and Aberavon clubs, a XV from Ebbw Vale and Abertillery, and a XV from Cross Keys, Pontypool and Newbridge. That sort of pattern continued until the 1970s. I'm sure that it was quite an honour to play against touring sides in this way, but playing for these combined teams wasn't quite the same as playing for your own club against some of the greats.

Following the Australia game, my next step was trying to win a place in the Wales team for the 1967 Five Nations tournament. This time I was chosen for the Probables trial team. The game was in Swansea,

I think. The only thing I can remember clearly was jumping for a line-out ball and my legs being knocked from underneath me again. I fell heavily on my shoulder and knocked it out of place. That was the end of the season for me, for both club and country. As it turned out, I didn't miss a particularly brilliant Wales Five Nations campaign that year. France won the Championship and we won't waste too much time discussing how Wales fared. Suffice to say that the only game we won was the one against England, 34–21.

But, for me, there was no more rugby in the 1966/67 season. It's very hard to accept a fact like that when all you want to do is play rugby. I'd been chosen for the Lions; I'd won my first cap for Wales and then, suddenly, everything came to a stop. That's quite a blow. I was taken to hospital to have my shoulder X-rayed. But I didn't have any special treatment just because I was a rugby player, I had to queue like everyone else. After confirming that the shoulder was dislocated, they put my arm in a sling and told me it would take seven weeks before it began to settle, so there was no point thinking of training before then. I had to let it heal naturally and wait for it to strengthen with time. The club played no part in the rehabilitation process in those days; it wasn't expected to. All the club told me was make sure that it healed properly and to return when it had. Again, how different to today, when players are sent to see specialists if they sneeze twice!

When I felt that things were beginning to improve,

I went to Carmarthen, to the Quins or the Athletic, to begin training again and play one or two games, before returning to Llanelli fully fit. I was away from work while injured too, but it was easier going back to work than it was returning to play rugby.

Local rivalries or bitter feuds, whichever you want to call them, are an integral part of rugby at every level. This is particularly true of Wales-England internationals on the one hand, and local town club rivalries on the other. But, as apparent as they are, I can't say that I fully understand them. The big rivalry in Carmarthen is between the Quins and the Athletic. As far as I'm aware, the Quins were the club which enjoyed great success in the town for many years. But, at the end of the Second World War, many men returned from the fighting but couldn't win their places back in the first XV. That didn't go down too well, so they formed their own team, Carmarthen Athletic. And that was the start of an intense rivalry that still continues today. I'm lucky to have good friends in both clubs and I've played for both as well. I don't understand why people can't just pull together more than they do.

Thank goodness, my injury was better by the time of Llanelli's next trip abroad, to Italy. We went out to the sunshine of Catania and Rome. If I'd heard of Germany and Berlin before going out there, I'd certainly heard of Rome, but in a different context altogether. Sunday school stories came back to my mind when I learned that we were going to Rome. Those New Testament stories that I'd heard in the chapel at Bancyfelin had given me a good grounding in the history of the place before arriving there, as, of course, had my actual history lessons in school. Once there, these stories came alive. That was particularly true of the Coliseum, which stood in magnificent splendour. It was quite an experience sitting in the Coliseum, and easy to imagine what had happened there during the period of those stories I remembered.

As the 1960s drew to a close, things were changing really quickly in Welsh rugby. In 1967 there was a notable change at the Llanelli club: a man called Ieuan Evans was chosen to be its first coach. That meant that the captain was no longer expected to take full charge of training and tactics; the coach would do that job now. That same year, the Wales team did the same, and appointed Dai Nash as its first coach. He was a former international and British Lion. The idea of coaches in rugby was beginning to spread for the first time.

Ieuan Evans came from the Betws area of Ammanford, and was the son of a coal miner. Like me, in his youth he loved football before he loved rugby. He played rugby between 1947 and 1958 for Ammanford, Neath, Llanelli and Swansea, before ending his career with the club where Shane Williams started his career, Amman United. He was a schoolteacher and this turned out to be a pattern in this new development of appointing coaches. Most of the early ones were schoolteachers, usually PE teachers. Ieuan continued to coach until he retired as a teacher in 1980. They were the amateur days, of course, and he didn't receive tuppence halfpenny for his work, not officially at least. He did receive official recognition for his services to rugby from one quarter, though. He was appointed a member of the Gorsedd of Bards at the National Eisteddfod in 1982, under the bardic name, Ieuan Morlais.

When Ieuan came to Stradey to coach, not only did he return to where he'd once played, but he was reunited with some faces that were familiar to him. In 1963, Ieuan was the first to be chosen to coach the Wales Youth team, a move instigated in order to close the gap between schools' rugby and first-class rugby. Under that system, he was responsible for developing the talents of players such as Phil Bennett, Derek Quinnell and Stuart Gallacher. Those three were to be an integral part of the Llanelli team on his watch in the years after the Wales Youth days. He also coached a young Ray Gravell too, but Ieuan had left by the time Grav joined the Scarlets.

Things changed when the coach was appointed. There was certainly less pressure on the captain. Instead of only one man keeping an eye on the backs and forwards, but never the two at the same time, the coach could watch everyone train and all XV play. I'm sure that this was laying the foundations for what was to follow at Llanelli.

On a personal level, as 1968 drew closer, there was good news for me once more. I'd been chosen for the Lions squad to tour South Africa. I was, understandably, absolutely delighted. I couldn't have asked for more. I had one Lions tour under my belt, but as far as Wales was concerned, I'd only played one game against Australia and three Five Nations games. That was the sum total of my international experience since returning from that first Lions tour. But the selectors were obviously happy with that. I did find it a little strange to prepare for my second Lions tour having only played four games for my country. However, I was looking forward to going to another country for the first time, with the pick of the British and Irish players. But the tour to South Africa was nothing like the tour of New Zealand in 1966.

8

Springboks

AT THE END of the 1960s I had a fairly clear understanding of what I might expect to see in South Africa. I'm not a very political person at all, I never have been. However, it was impossible not to know what was going in that part of the world at the time. The news was full of apartheid-related stories. Nelson Mandela had been incarcerated, and in 1968 there was the big fuss about the cricketer, Basil D'Oliveira. He was South African-born, but not a white man, he was coloured. He'd represented England at cricket, but wasn't chosen to go on their tour of South Africa for fear of the animosity that that would cause out there. However, another player was injured, and Basil was called up. The South African authorities refused to accept an England squad which included D'Oliveira and a serious row between the two countries ensued. In the end, a compromise wasn't possible, so the whole tour was cancelled. And into such a climate we'd be arriving.

There wasn't much public discussion as to whether the Lions should go on tour or not. The apartheid argument hadn't really gripped our sport at that time.

However, individual players did discuss the issue, and rugby's role in it. I think the consensus was that rugby and politics didn't mix and we were only there to play rugby matches. Many sports people held that view, even when the whole issue became a lot more intense a few years later.

We did travel to South Africa and, for me personally, it was the sixth or seventh country rugby had taken me to in a matter of a few years. The first thing that struck me on arrival was how rich the country was. I was familiar with the black pyramids of coal in the Cross Hands region of Carmarthenshire in the 1950s and 1960s, but out there, they were pyramids of gold. And that's what my first impression was, not the issue of black and white and apartheid. I expected to see a society with two types of people, differentiated by their skin colour. But I didn't, at first. The division I saw was between the very rich and the very poor. As time went on I did become more aware of the plight of the black people, and witnessing the way that they lived really shook me. You wouldn't keep chickens or pigs in those conditions back home. The difference in the way we were treated as a squad, and the way the black people were treated, couldn't have been further apart. A few of us went on an unofficial visit to the Soweto Township, so that we could see for ourselves. I really can't begin to describe the things we saw there. I haven't got the words.

We were treated like kings in every hotel we went to. But once we stepped out of those hotels of an evening, it was a horrible experience to see how many people lived in the doorways of shops. Whole families lived in cardboard boxes. During the day, the sight that horrified me was that of little children scurrying through the city traffic, barefoot, wearing skimpy vests that hung on their bony frames. I do find it difficult to describe what I saw and even more difficult to say how that affected me. All I can say is that what you see in person with your own eyes is nothing like what you see on television. Thoughts of village life in Bancyfelin came to me very regularly when I saw what life was like for most people out there.

I remember going into a shop in Johannesburg where there were people queuing in front of me, waiting to be served. They were all black people. The shopkeeper called me to the front, but I refused, saying that the people in front of me should be seen to first. She became quite indignant and insisted that I went to the front of the queue and be served before everyone else. That was a horrible feeling.

Some time later, three or four of us went out for a meal in Port Elizabeth. Just outside our hotel, on the way back, we saw a black man whose banger of a car had broken down. It was obvious that the battery was flat. We approached him and offered to bump start his car. We told him to jump behind the steering wheel and we'd push. The car started instantly and the man stepped out of his car, ran over to us, obviously amazed at what we'd done. He fell on his knees before us and thanked us profusely.

Back in the hotel, a man behind the reception desk, having seen the incident, called us over, obviously very angry.

'You shouldn't have done that!'

'Why?' I asked him back.

'You shouldn't have done what you've just done. We don't do things like that out here!'

'Put it like this,' I answered further, 'if it was you in that car, wouldn't you be glad if someone helped you to get it going again?'

He didn't reply. Hearing the way he spoke to us was certainly shocking. So too was seeing buses for black people only and other buses for whites only. At another time, a group of us players went to play golf. One of the boys, David Brooks, was having a particularly bad day, having lost many golf balls on his way round. Finally, having had enough, he turned to his caddy, a black man, and said, mocking himself as he did so:

'Hey, you have a go!'

'No boss. I'll lose my job if I do that!'

We didn't expect such an answer. David then insisted that he had a go. Eventually, the black caddy did, sending the ball sweetly down the fairway in a way that David could only stand and admire. Those of us Lions who were there then discussed at length what we'd seen. We were all in agreement: if men and boys like him were given the opportunity to develop their talent, that would be of benefit not only to the individual, but to the country as a whole. But, of course, they were never going to be given any opportunity. And all this was going on in a country that was *theirs* in the first place.

Halfway through the tour we had a five-day break in the game reserve of the Kruger National Park. That was a fantastic experience, especially as we were staying in straw huts. We'd get up at five in the morning so that we could witness what people in the park called 'The Kill'. That's when animals of prey, such as lions, go out hunting before sunrise, before it gets too hot. It was really exciting to be within 20 yards of a lion catching another animal. I'll never forget being out in the middle of the African plain and seeing it red in tooth and claw. After all, it was the natural life cycle of the countryside, just like back home but with some obvious differences!

But there was a shadow hanging over that excursion, too. We came across a group of around 30 to 40 black men thrashing the bamboo undergrowth near a river which was full of crocodiles. Many of the men worked very close to the water and, at times, had to even wade into it. In charge of them was a white Afrikaner, gun in hand:

'Aren't you at risk from the crocodiles?' I asked him.

'Oh, yes,' he replied, 'that's why I've got the gun.'

'But do some of the men get killed?'

'I don't know,' he said back to me, 'we don't bother to count them when they come back.'

Those horrible, inhuman words were a disgrace to hear.

On the way back from Kruger we travelled in

separate cars, with about five players and a driver in each. Through the car windows we could see dozens of children at the side of the road. They were about five, six or seven years old, standing there on their own, with no adult in sight. Having seen many such groups of children, I asked the driver why they were there.

'Oh, take no notice,' he said, 'the fathers send children out from the villages to the roadside to sell some things they've made so they can get a bit of money.'

I asked him to stop the car the next time he saw such a group of children. We passed quite few more groups, but the driver wouldn't stop. We persuaded him in the end and he did stop. He still insisted on making his point however, and refused to stop right next to the one solitary child he'd seen, choosing to park some way further up the road instead. As we walked from the car towards the boy, he ran towards the fence behind him. He got himself stuck and we could see a frightened look in his eyes. We asked him what was wrong, but, of course, he didn't understand us. The driver asked him and the child replied. He thought that we were the police, as it was against the law for him to be doing what he was doing, so he'd tried to flee. He accepted that we weren't policemen and eventually opened his bag for us to see what he had inside. He had animal figures carved from wood. Each one of us players bought a carving from him and, as a result, the boy was given a lot of money. We also shared the sweets and oranges we had with us. He put his money and the other gifts in his bag, with a massive smile on his face that suggested he'd just received great treasure. He ran back through the undergrowth towards his home as fast as his little legs could carry him, no doubt to share the spoils of the day proudly with his family.

I bought a bird carving from him. We've moved house three times since I came back from that tour of South Africa and that little bird has moved with me each time. I'll never throw it out because it reminds me of that little boy by the side of the road. When I see the bird on the shelf, I often think what became of that little boy. The answer, more than likely, is that he is no longer alive.

Another thing I remember from that trip was being at the Newlands Stadium, Cape Town, and meeting the first man ever to receive a heart transplant. South African Dr Christiaan Barnard performed the first ever heart transplant at Groote Schuur Hospital, Cape Town, some months prior to our visit. Both surgeon and patient, Louis Washkansky, came to the famous sports stadium to meet us. It was quite a sight to see a man who'd just received a new heart standing on the pitch throwing a rugby ball back and forth with some of us. But we weren't allowed to shake hands with him or touch him in any way.

The rugby itself was different out there too compared to what we'd experienced in New Zealand. The air was a lot thinner and the pitches much harder as a result. We forwards certainly felt it when we collapsed in a heap on the ground. We might well

Three brothers – Eddie, Dai and me

Me and Eddie at Number 14, Bancyfelin

Me at the beginning of the 1940s

Lifting weights at home in Bancyfelin – I've still got those weights!

Playing for St Clears youth team at the end of the 1950s

My response after I heard that I'd be touring with the Lions for the first time!

Starting the celebrations after succeeding to get into the house, at last!

A presentation from the Chairman of the Electricity Board after my selection to play for the Lions

Those budgies I worried so much about before going on the Lions tour

My first Lions shirt

Departing for five months overseas with the Lions in 1966, with just one suitcase and a kit bag!

Celebrations at Bancyfelin hall in 1966, with C.L. Davies, the first one from the village to win an international cap, on the right

A Lion astride a horse in South Africa

My first cap for my country

Brian Price congratulates me on my selection to play in his place (due to injury) for Wales in 1969 – the Triple Crown match against England. The young Gareth Edwards keeps an eye on us!

Playing against Fiji on the return from Wales' tour to New Zealand in 1969

Receiving a warm welcome from the people and Mayor of Carmarthen after the successful Lions tour to New Zealand in 1971

On the balcony of Carmarthen's town hall on the same occasion

Me, Roy Mathias, Phil Bennett, Roy Bergiers and Derek Quinnell on the way to South Africa with Llanelli in 1972

With some of the Llanelli boys on the way to South Africa

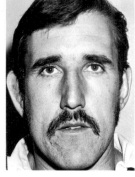

Pen pic from the programme of the All Blacks game in 1972

The master, Carwyn James

A rare colour photograph of the Llanelli game with the All Blacks in 1972

Opening a petrol station in Llanelli shortly after defeating the All Blacks

Llanelli's first Union Cup in 1973

Another cup!

One of the 454 games for Llanelli

Yet another cup!

My mother and
stepfather, 1950

Eddie, Uncle Glyn
– who was in the Navy
– and granddad

Me and Eddie at the wedding of
our sister, Pamela

Bethan and me just before our marriage, about 1963

From the left, my sisters Beryl and Pamela, my brother Eddie, me, my mother and my stepfather

My grandmother and my grandfather at their golden wedding celebration at the Mansel Arms, Carmarthen

Our wedding day at St Peter's
Church, Carmarthen, 1967

With the family at Amroth, and starting to
enjoy my retirement from rugby

With Tracy

Enjoying time in Canada with Bethan
after retiring from work

With the family after retirement
from rugby – at our former home
in Johnstown

Visiting a coral reef on a trip to
Australia to visit my uncle

The family – me, Tracy and her son Robert, Bethan and Helen

Robert and me on a beach in Pembrokeshire

Roy Bergiers and me meeting Scottish Lion, Gordon Brown, at the Ivy Bush, Carmarthen

An opportunity to meet Bryan Williams, president of New Zealand Rugby Union and a member of the All Blacks in 1972, at a celebration dinner in 2012

The best Lion of them all, Willie John McBride, outside the Brangwyn Hall, Swansea, at the time of the memorial service for Mervyn Davies

Great enjoyment at Parc y Scarlets: a charity dinner with Gareth, Clive, Phil and Roy, 2012

Being admitted to the Gorsedd of Bards at the National Eisteddfod in Llanelli, 2000

A dear friend

Four Lions in the Gorsedd: Terry Davies, Clive Rowlands, Grav and me

have hit the ground hard, but it was the ground that left its mark on us! If we were injured in any way, the referees had a different attitude. No-one was allowed to run on with a sponge and some water to help us; it was a case of 'get on your feet and get on with the game'! Our coach came onto the pitch in one game to give one of the boys some water because he was injured. The referee sent him off straight away. It didn't matter that the temperature was in the 80s Fahrenheit and that we were playing at altitude. We were only allowed water at half-time. In order to help us play in such conditions, we had to take salt tablets once a day because we were perspiring so much. I'll never forget those tablets, either. They were massive, about the size of half a crown and very difficult to swallow.

In the Orange Free State, as the name implies, they grow oranges everywhere. Our game there was a very difficult one, and quite a dirty game, to be honest. When one of our boys fell to the ground injured not far from the touchline, a sack full of these oranges came in handy, as some fans showered us with oranges and various other fruit as well. Willie John would then take us out to the centre of the pitch, so that we were further from the fans.

The game in Springs has taken its place in the annals of Lions history, but not for a good reason. One of our props on that tour was Welshman John O'Shea. He was quite a character on the field, and off it as well, and he could be a little too handy with his fists. He was sent off in that game, the first Lion to be ordered off for foul play. Just before he was dismissed, one of our players had to leave the field because he had broken a bone in his hand. It was that kind of game! I then moved to play prop instead of John. Luckily, I had experience of playing prop for the Lions in New Zealand. John was banned for two games after that. He was still a valuable player to have on the tour, making us all laugh at every possible opportunity. On one plane journey, John went to the cockpit to speak to the pilot. He grabbed the microphone and addressed the passengers:

'This is your captain speaking! We will be landing in [whichever airport it was] airport – or thereabouts – in about half an hour or so!'

Everybody looked confused because he'd said 'thereabouts' and 'or so' but we knew exactly what was going on! His son is just the same as him – Rick O'Shea, who comments on rugby for the BBC.

I wasn't chosen to play in the first two Test matches. But I was chosen for the third Test – as a prop. I played in that position in the fourth Test, too. I was becoming an experienced British Lions prop!

Black people were allowed to come and watch our matches, but they were kept in one place, together, behind a massive wire fence that was about 40 feet high. They were, to all intents and purposes, in a cage. The blacks were always supportive and that was just about the only backing we received as British Lions out there. Every time our full back Bob Hiller kicked a conversion or penalty, they would roar enthusiastically. Bob would play up to that and would turn to acknowledge their appreciation of his play. He didn't care if he was offending the hosts by recognising the presence of the black people. That wasn't the point for him, no more than it was for the rest of us.

Being in South Africa was a very uncomfortable experience. There was always a shadow hanging over everything. We enjoyed the rugby, that's certain. But seeing how the black people were treated would turn our stomachs often. Things have changed by now, of course. But I still say that New Zealand is my favourite country of all those that I've played rugby in.

9

Gumshields

THE 1960S WERE a time of tremendous change in all areas of society, including rugby, even if the rest of the world hadn't noticed. A great deal happened in the game that decade and the legacy of those changes is still to be seen today.

Within a period of twelve months, I fell under the influence of two very special men who left their mark on Welsh rugby. Clive Rowlands took over as the Wales national coach for the first time on the tour of Argentina in 1968, taking full charge of the team for the Five Nations Championship the following year. Also in 1969, Carwyn James took charge at Llanelli when Ieuan Evans departed. By the end of the decade therefore, I was being coached by two rugby giants. Both men would go on to be extremely successful, but in different ways.

That same year, Clive took the Wales squad on a tour of New Zealand. It was the first overseas tour where caps would be awarded for Test matches. No caps had been given on the Wales tour of Argentina a year earlier. Caps, until then, had only been earned if you played against one of the other Five Nations, or the three southern hemisphere nations at home. Out in New Zealand in 1969, we didn't lose a single regional game but we lost both Tests. I wasn't selected for the first Test but I played in the second, as a result of an injury to Brian Thomas. It was really nice to be back in that country and experience the warmth of its people once more.

On the way home we stopped off in Australia and played a Test match in Sydney. We won that game, 19–16, thanks to tries by Gerald Davies, Dai Morris and John Taylor, with the other points coming from the boot of centre Keith Jarrett. Gerald's try was scored from the wing – he was playing in that position for the first time on the tour. Clive Rowlands thought that Gerald needed to be moved from the centre and out wide. What a wise decision! That's the last time Wales beat Australia away – a record I'd be more than happy to see go!

After Sydney our tour was still not over. There was one further stop, Fiji. We were to play against the national team in Suva, with no caps for this game, either. We won comfortably enough, 31–11, even though it was 8–8 at half-time. Our number 8, Dennis Hughes, scored three tries, with Maurice Richards and John Taylor scoring a try apiece. Jarrett kicked five conversions and JPR dropped a goal. One thing stands out as I think back to the Fiji visit – the heat! It was so hot, and humid with it, too. But, once again, the people were wonderful, so friendly.

We arrived back home having enjoyed that tour very much. This was only the second 'official' tour by Wales to the southern hemisphere. The first had visited South Africa in 1964, with Clive Rowlands as captain. They played one game against South Africa and three regional games before stopping off in Kenya to play an Eastern Africa team. All that was so new in those days, of course, and it was the beginning of a pattern that still exists to this day. The rugby world was slowly expanding and developing.

As I've mentioned already, the whole idea of coaching was certainly in its infancy then. Before Dai Nash took charge of Wales and Ieuan Evans came to Llanelli, many had been calling for a Wales national coach, and for coaches to have an input at clubs, too. Their point was that coaching occurred throughout the schools' system but it stopped once your education had finished and, ironically, stopped if you played for a first-class team, including your national team. Change did happen thank goodness, and I was lucky to be a beneficiary of that change. It was a privilege to be there at the start of a new chapter in the history of Welsh rugby.

Little did I know then that Clive and Carwyn would generate so much discussion and disagreement in the Welsh rugby fraternity, both by organisers and fans. Now, looking back, I can see that both men had their virtues. Their styles were completely different, however. Clive was one of us, one of the boys. He'd had a long career playing for clubs in Wales and the national team. He was chosen as captain of Wales the very first time he played for his country. In fact, he was captain every time he played for Wales! Quite an achievement! He lived the international rugby world as one of the boys on the pitch.

Carwyn was quite different. He'd played rugby and he'd been capped. However, he never broke through as a player, living as he did in the shadow of the great outside-half, Cliff Morgan. Carwyn, like Clive, was a teacher. But he was a teacher at a public school, and then went on to be a college lecturer. Their personalities were so different, too. Clive, as I said, was one of us and that didn't change when he started coaching. I had nothing to say against Clive then and I haven't now. Carwyn, on the other hand, was quieter, more introverted, and thoughtful. An extremely likeable man, but not one we'd share things with as we did with Clive. But again, I had nothing to say against him then and I haven't now. Discussions about the merits of the two are often lost in the mists of time. Incidentally, they both got on with each other very well.

The two of them had similarities, too. When Clive started coaching Wales, he told us quite clearly that he was the only one who would conduct press interviews. And as different as their personalities were, that's exactly what Carwyn told us too. I often think of that when I see today's players being interviewed after the match. I don't think that either Clive or Carwyn would have been to happy with that. On that point, I'll never forget one of Clive's first press interviews after being chosen as Wales coach. Questions were being asked about a recent Wales performance and the merits, or otherwise, of players. One journalist started his question, 'The experts are saying...'

But before he could finish, Clive cut across him. 'Who exactly are these experts then? Can you tell me?'

The journalist shut up instantly. We were more than happy to leave press questioning to Clive; he knew how to handle them. If a blunt answer wasn't necessary, Clive had no shortage of funny and colourful anecdotes to keep every press conference entertained. Carwyn had his way of dealing with the public face of the game, too. He was just as clever as Clive, but his method was different. No-one ever asked Carwyn any awkward questions in the first place, as they knew they wouldn't get the answer they wanted. Carwyn was master of the short, concise answer that went straight to the core of the issue at hand. He had the ability to think deeper than those asking him questions.

The development of the role of a rugby coach and the whole idea of rugby journalists being able to question coaches about the game progressed side by side. Clive and Carwyn were there at the start and could handle these new questioners and they enjoyed the theatre of the whole thing.

I can't help but think that these two characters would have a lot to say about the game today. Modern rugby coaching academies seem to churn out coach after coach who are all the same. There's not much room for individuality today. Do those who run the game today have new ideas, as their 1960s counterparts did, ones that can be seen on the field? I'm not too sure. Little wonder then that today's game has become boring, in my opinion.

Carwyn's early days with Llanelli changed things a lot for us players. We'd started to get used to the whole idea of being coached, thanks to Ieuan. But Carwyn was so different. We learned a lot about rugby from him, changing the way we thought about the game as a whole. His way of doing so was very simple. When we'd be out on the field, going through some training move or other, he'd regularly stop the play, and turn to an individual player and ask, 'Why did you do that?'

That sounds so simple and basic. But nobody had asked us that before. His aim was simple. He wanted us to think for ourselves, to ask ourselves why we'd done what we'd just done – the things that we'd done instinctively for so long but without knowing why. We hadn't considered whether there was another way of doing the same.

On the field of play, Carwyn had one pet hate – kicking the ball into the opposition's half. He didn't see any point to it. He preferred the outside-half, or whoever, to place a much shorter kick just over the heads of the line of defence. This would force the full back to come forward and force the other backs to turn round and run back. He saw no point in kicking long, right into the full back's hands so that he could clear downfield and make us turn to run back downfield. He'd be really annoyed if that happened.

'For goodness sake, you're playing really well and working hard to win the ball and then you kick the bloody thing away!'

We'd hear that often. We still hear the same cry today from frustrated fans, if not so much from coaches.

When Carwyn arrived at Llanelli he was by then a lecturer at Trinity College, Carmarthen. It wasn't unusual to see him arrive straight from lectures, a little late for training. On those occasions he'd had no time to change into his tracksuit. He'd stand on the touchline in his suit and tie, but his trouser bottoms would be tucked into his socks, with rugby togs on his feet. And, of course, a Senior Service cigarette between his fingers.

The training sessions changed completely. They were carefully thought-out beforehand and he knew exactly what he wanted to do in each. For one thing, he started what he called clinics, when he'd take groups of players aside – the halfbacks for example, or the back row – and go through things with them in a very specialised way. He also knew how to use others to bring out the best in his players. He made good use of Norman Gale and Tom Hudson, both of whom knew more about forward play and fitness, respectively, than he did. He certainly was quite happy to delegate if that was necessary. He didn't have a fear of letting go. He knew how to get the best out of people and his man management skills were second to none.

It was during Carwyn's time that I first sat down to watch films of other teams playing, as part of a training session. We'd watch these games and Carwyn would stop the film now and again to highlight some point or other. One thing that was an obvious feature of these sessions was that when he did stop the film, it was invariably to highlight the weaknesses of the team being analysed. Their strengths were obvious, he'd say, we didn't need to concentrate on them. But we needed to look at where they were weak and think about those areas.

He taught us all, every one of the XV on the pitch, how to use the length and breadth of the field, emphasising at the same time that we should let the ball do all the work as we played the wide game.

In 1969, it was still within the rules to kick the ball directly into touch from anywhere on the pitch. There's one famous example of a rather vigorous use of this tactic, back at the start of the 1960s, which brings Clive Rowlands back into the story. In 1963, when Wales were playing Scotland on a really muddy pitch, Clive decided to kick the ball out of play at every possible opportunity – the reason being to help Wales secure the slender advantage they had in the match. As a result of Clive's tactics, the game records 111 line-outs! They say that outside-half Dai Watkins only touched the ball about five times throughout the whole game! I'm so glad that I wasn't playing in that one! Despite that, the law wasn't changed until

1970, allowing kicking directly to touch only from within the 25-yard line.

That's the kind of time it was, with many changes happening on and off the field. Some changes weren't quite so successful and I'm thinking about another line-out-related change in particular. The idea of double-banking was introduced. In other words, both teams had two lines in a line-out. How ridiculous was that? Four lines of players waiting for the throw in! Thank goodness that didn't last long.

A little later, at the end of the 1972/73 season, a far more sensible line-out change was introduced – the one about maintaining a set distance between the two lines and between the individual players in each line. Before then, if you notice in the pictures from that time, there was no rule as to where we had to stand. There was an awful lot of bunching going on! I'll never forget Scott Quinnell, after seeing a photo of his father Derek in a line-out, asking him, 'How the hell did you have any room to jump?'

Nobody was allowed to lift another player; every forward had to jump under his own steam. The touch judge wasn't allowed to intervene in any way, either. As I said earlier, the referee really was all on his own. So, of course, he didn't see everything that happened, especially in the line-outs and scrums. Thank goodness, the referee can get help from the touchlines today and, of course, from the TMO.

Without such extra assistance, off the ball incidents were so much more difficult to see. If the referee moved along with play, he'd often have to leave a heap of bodies behind him. They could do what they wanted in that heap, as the referee was far away. Kick-offs were interesting times too, either at the start of a game or at any re-start during it. There was nothing either to stop opposing players running straight at you as you rose to catch the ball, and clatter you to the ground like a sack of spuds. I broke many a rib that way. Feet don't go into rucks now as they used to. In fact, that sort of rucking doesn't happen these days. And one more thing, there was no penalty for a high tackle. Thank goodness, we didn't have yellow or red cards then, either!

With all that in mind, when people challenge me today saying that I wouldn't last the full 80 minutes in the modern game, my answer is simple. The game today is cleaner than it has ever been. The increased power of the officials, the television coverage, and law changes have led to much less foul play than there used to be. Maybe the hits are harder, but the game is a lot less dangerous than it used to be. I'm glad that players are allowed to wear protective gear these days. When I go to see school children play rugby now, and see what they have under their jerseys, it makes me smile when I think back to that referee in New Zealand telling me to take a piece of sponge out from under my jersey. His words, 'You're either fit to play or you're not!' ring in my mind.

Carwyn introduced one other big change at Llanelli at the start of the 1970s. He met us as a squad one training night and asked if any of us had ever considered wearing gumshields. We all looked in amazement at each other. 'Only boxers wore gumshields' is what we were all thinking, I'm sure. Why would we need one? In my case, I'd been on two Lions tours without having to wear one. But, of course, they were introduced at Llanelli. Carwyn asking the question was a fair indication that he already thought they were needed. Once we got used to them, we wondered how on the earth we'd played without them up until then.

It certainly was a period of change. The game was taking its first steps into the modern era. Carwyn was centre stage. After his arrival at Llanelli, things were never quite the same again. That was evident to everyone. But, not one of us who was at Stradey at the time could ever have imagined that there was so much more to come from Carwyn and the club, and that that would be on the world stage.

10

Forty-five per cent

I DIDN'T PLAY a full Five Nations Championship until 1970, four years after winning my first cap. I came close in 1968, playing three games. However, I only managed one the following year, the match when we easily beat England. It was, therefore, a rather nice feeling to play four games in 1970, especially since we won three of them, losing only to Ireland. We shared the Championship with France that year. But it was the game against England that was the one to remember, as it so often is, but for a unique reason this time.

The game was played at Twickenham and it's a definite milestone in the history of rugby. The referee, Robert Calmet from France, sustained an injury, so the Englishman Johnny Johnson came on instead of him. Then, Gareth Edwards was injured and Chico Hopkins replaced him. Chico had an excellent game, creating a try for JPR and then scoring one himself, which secured a Welsh victory after Wales had been behind for most of the game. That was the first time a substitute had scored a try in an international.

It's also the only time Gareth failed to finish an international match in his career.

Playing for Wales in the Five Nations meant that I missed one really important game for my club. In January 1970, Llanelli were to play South Africa at Stradey. They were visiting Wales at a very exciting time for rugby generally, and Llanelli in particular, as Carwyn James had just taken over. Changes weren't in full swing yet however, and the preparation for the South Africa game was the same as for any other. It was nothing like the way we prepared for the All Blacks game two years later. The club, nor the town itself, warmed to the Springbok visit in the way they would to the All Blacks later on. But we'll come to that soon enough.

Carwyn's preparation was still extremely thorough of course, as we'd come to expect. But there was one difference. When it was kick-off time, Carwyn wasn't in his usual seat. He was strongly opposed to the apartheid system in South Africa. By 1970, the situation had escalated considerably since our visit out there with the Lions two years earlier. It was so much more of a political hot potato in the sporting world now than in 1968. Carwyn was of the opinion that opposition to apartheid should be shown at every possible opportunity. Consequently, when he learned that the club had arranged a fixture on South Africa's tour in 1969/70, Carwyn agreed to prepare the team for the game but decided that he wouldn't watch it. When the players took to the field, Carwyn disappeared from the public arena completely. The story is that he sat under the stand listening to the game on the radio. Whatever he did, he'd made his point and everyone in the rugby world knew that.

I wasn't allowed to play in the game anyway, neither was Phil Bennett. The rule in those days was that if you were selected to play for Wales, you couldn't turn out for your club within five days of an impending international. Wales were to play South Africa on a Saturday, therefore playing for Llanelli on the Tuesday before wasn't possible. Phil and I sat in the stand to watch Llanelli vs South Africa, and we very nearly beat them. They won by a single point, with a last-minute conversion attempt by us just failing to go over. That conversion followed one of the best tries that Llanelli has ever scored – very similar to the famous Barbarian try against the All Blacks in 1973. Alan Richards grounded the ball after almost every player in the team had handled it along the way. That was certainly an early indication of the style of rugby Carwyn wanted to develop at the club.

Not long after that, it was announced that Carwyn was to be the coach of the Lions tour to New Zealand the following year. He went from being a club coach to a Lions coach in one step, without coaching his country first. Llanelli played against English teams such as Wasps, Saracens, London Welsh, Harlequins, Northampton, Moseley, Bristol, and so on. The organisers of the game in England would have seen enough evidence of the way Carwyn worked to know his attributes and how he wanted to develop the game. But, that said, he still hadn't proved himself on an international stage before he left for the Land of the Long White Cloud.

However, before that we had to take part in the 1971 Five Nations Championship – one that would prove to be special for the Welsh. For the second year in a row, I played all four matches in the Five Nations. We won the Grand Slam that year, the first time since 1952. The squad was certainly pulling together and starting to show the style of play that would become so dominant in the years to come. One of those matches has stayed in the memory of all Welsh fans who saw it, I'm sure. We played Scotland at Murrayfield. As the game was drawing to a close, Scotland were ahead 18–14, following a Chris Rea try. Peter Brown missed the conversion, but they still had a four-point lead going into the last few minutes. We won a line-out and I tapped the ball back to Gareth Edwards, who then threw it out to Barry John, who passed it to John Dawes, he found JPR who'd come into the line, and he passed the ball to Gerald Davies who went round the Scottish defence to score in the corner. We were a point behind now, with the conversion to come. Our flanker, John Taylor, stepped up to take the kick. He'd scored a lovely try right at the start of the game, and now he had the opportunity to win the game outright with a kick at the end. The conversion was on the right-hand side of the pitch for left-footed John. Despite being wide out on the touchline, John's kick sailed through the middle of the posts and we'd won, 19–18. That was quite a game, full of excitement and tension, and a victory for us at the end.

Within a matter of months, the Lions were aboard a plane to New Zealand. Little wonder, after our Five Nations success, that many of those seats were occupied by Welshmen. And, of course, a Welshman was coaching us, so he'd know all the Welsh players' game very well. But there were still some who whinged a little bit because there were too many Welshmen on the tour, just as they did in 2013 when the Lions went to Australia.

Once out there, Carwyn's coaching methods didn't change one bit as he dealt with players from four different nations. He'd deal with each person as an individual and work out what that person needed. Some would need words of encouragement; others would need a kick up the backside. Carwyn knew who needed what.

Many times on tour we'd be on a coach travelling to our next destination, with Carwyn moving around and sitting next to different players, having a chat with them. Quite often, those conversations involved Carwyn telling a player that he needn't train that day. He'd have noticed that such and such was looking a little jaded or stale and he'd decide that they'd benefit more from rest than training.

As he did at Llanelli, he'd also have a chat with individual players on a more informal basis of an evening. This was especially true of the Welsh-speaking members of that Lions tour. He'd like to keep in touch with his roots and be reminded of home comforts, and talking to some of us in his native tongue was an obvious way of doing that. If this happened later in the evening, then the inevitable bottle of wine would appear. If Barry, Gerald, Gareth, Geoff Evans, Derek Quinnell, and myself were with him, the conversation would flow with the wine, or a soft drink in my case. If ever Willie John McBride was around on such occasions, he'd come across and comment about us speaking in a language no-one else understood. But really he was just teasing. As an Irishman, he could understand what was going on, if not the language.

Carwyn never hid his politics if there was an occasion to discuss such matters. We all knew that after his stand against apartheid during the Llanelli vs South Africa game. He stood as the Plaid Cymru candidate in the Llanelli by-election of 1970. He suggested to me that he thought that might have jeopardised his chances of coaching the Lions, as he'd stated clearly that he was a candidate in that election. He was obviously still chosen for the Lions. When we congregated in Eastbourne, he shared his views with us there as well. But, however ready he was to share his politics, he never forced his views on anyone.

I remember one of these conversations with Carwyn. We were talking about rugby that time, not politics, and he touched on the type of thinking that led him to sit next to players on the team coach offering advice.

He said, '*Ti'n gweld, gall unrhyw un roi sosban ddŵr*

ar y tân a'i berwi'n sych. Ond y gamp yw rhoi'r sosban ar y tân a'i chadw i ffrwtian cyn hired ag sy'n bosib gan wbod pryd mae dod â hi 'nôl i'r berw unwaith 'to. Sdim diben cael chwaraewyr sydd 120 y cant yn ffit yn gorfforol ond eu meddyliau wedi blino.' ['Anyone can put a saucepan full of water on the fire and boil it dry. The trick is to put the saucepan on the fire and keep it simmering for as long as possible and then bring it back to the boil again. It's of no use at all to have a player 120 per cent physically fit, but with their minds tired.']

And, of course, he was perfectly correct. His skill was knowing which of the players were near to boiling dry and then tell them before it actually happened.

I don't think New Zealand rugby quite knew what to make of this 'unknown' in charge of the Lions. They didn't have much of a clue who he was before he arrived. He certainly aroused their curiosity. There would be a gang of reporters at each training session. Sometimes, in order to confuse them a little, Carwyn would walk out onto the training ground with cricket gear. Then, as a British and Irish Lions rugby squad, we'd play a game of cricket in the full glare of very perplexed New Zealand rugby reporters! At other times, he'd decide to have a game of football during a training session. Carwyn knew exactly what he was doing, of course. He was keeping the opposition on their toes, causing a certain degree of confusion and uncertainty. Then, less frequently, he'd bring an intense training session to a premature end and tell us all to go and play a round of golf. As well as playing tricks with the opposition, these tactics also brought us closer together as a squad.

One game from that tour remains in my mind to this day, apart from the Test matches, of course: the Canterbury game before the first Test. That was, without doubt, the dirtiest game I've ever played in. Carwyn obviously expected a tough game; he pulled Barry John to one side and told him that he wasn't going to play. He feared that Barry would be a sitting target for the Canterbury forwards, who would probably do all they could to stop our star outside-half playing in the first Test. It was a wise move. We lost three players to injury in that game, sustained by what can only be called dubious play: McLoughlin, Carmichael and Hipwell. It was a huge loss, especially losing two props. But thanks to Carwyn's foresight Barry was saved for the Test. I was just glad to get to the end of the game and really glad that I had a gumshield!

Barry was the obvious star of the tour. That's when he was first called 'King', in response to the way he ruled play with his skilful running and kicking. It was no coincidence that Carwyn and Barry were such good friends. Carwyn understood him. In the changing rooms, before a game, Carwyn or John Dawes, the captain, would run through some moves they expected to see in the game ahead. As far as the backs were concerned, John Dawes explained there would probably only be two or three particular moves. Carwyn would then reinforce what had been said, making sure that we understood the instructions. Barry would inevitably open his mouth: 'Yes, OK, I understand these moves. And you can call whatever move you want. But if you call a certain move and I can see a gap somewhere, I'm bloody going for it!'

And Carwyn would stand there smiling quietly to himself, winking at some of us, as if to say that he understood exactly what Barry meant and he wasn't going to stand in his way. It needed a mind like Carwyn's to understand a mind like Barry's. Carwyn brought the natural creativity out of him, as a good coach should do. He didn't expect a talent like Barry's to play slavishly to a pre-planned system that could have destroyed individuality. And there is room for that in a team game.

Off the field, Carwyn also knew how to handle the players. He was more than willing for the boys to have a pint or two but he'd always emphasise that we should be sensible about it. If anyone overstepped the mark, Carwyn would make a note of it. But he wouldn't say anything straight away. He'd go up to his room at the end of the night, winking at one or two of us, as if to say that he'd seen what had gone on, and would deal with it the following day in his own way. The following morning, at the end of the training session, we'd make our way back to the changing rooms. But then Carwyn's voice would be heard, calling back two or three players who'd overstepped the mark the night before. Their training session hadn't come to the end. No player would be a repeat offender, and that out of respect for Carwyn, not fear of him.

As a fervent chapelgoer himself, Carwyn would respect any player's wish to go to church on Sundays. He'd do so himself, whenever the opportunity arose. Not many of us went to a service on Sunday, but one squad member did. Sean Lynch was a committed Catholic who would go to Mass whenever he could. It didn't matter how heavy the Saturday night had been, he'd be up and about ready for Mass in the morning. Then, back he'd come to the hotel, into our midst with a wide grin on his face: 'I've wiped the slate clean, boys! I can start all over again!'

If ever we were travelling on a coach that same Sunday, Carwyn would stand up at some point and turn to face the players, asking us mischievously enough: 'Anyone been to church today then, boys?'

He knew full well that it was only Sean who had been. Sean would then be forced to stand up as the rest of us teased him mercilessly. Sean had bad bouts of homesickness and Carwyn's goading of him was a way thought to bring him more into the fold.

Every evening, on the occasion of the squad dinner, Carwyn would invite two players to sit with him and manager Doug Smith at the top table. Doug was the opposite of Carwyn, a very impetuous man who could lose his cool easily. When this would happen, Carwyn often turned to me, saying more than once, *''Edrycha ar y dyn dwl!'* ['Look at the silly man!'] The custom at the dinner table was that Carwyn and Doug would choose the wine alternately. Carwyn really did know his wine. Doug thought that he did. Carwyn knew otherwise: '*So hwn yn deall dim am win. Mae'n meddwl bod e ond does dim syniad 'da fe!*' ['He doesn't understand anything about wine. He thinks he does, but he hasn't got a clue!']

We heard that so often! I remember one night, when I was at their table, that it was Doug's turn to choose the wine. Carwyn took one sip and turned to me in disgust: 'Oh dear. Bloody Tovali!' Tovali being a brand of pop made by a Carmarthen-based company and very popular in south Wales!

Whenever on tour, Carwyn would make sure that he had time to go shopping for one person in particular. Norah Isaac was a well-known and influential figure in Welsh academic and literary circles. She taught with Carwyn at Trinity College, and was a likeable lady but not one to cross lightly. She had influence in the college, which Carwyn realised, of course. I saw him coming back from a shopping trip one day in New Zealand. He showed me that he'd bought a gift, 'something small' as he said, but a gift that would help to keep her sweet so that he could have more of his way at the college.

As it happened, Norah Isaac lived next door to my brother in Carmarthen. One day, when I went to see him, she called me over.

'*Mae'r dyn 'na Carwyn, wel, weles i neb yn debyg iddo fe. 'Na'r unig ddyn yn 'y mywyd i sy'n gallu gwneud beth fynno fe â fi!*' ['That man Carwyn James! I never saw anyone like him. He's the only man in my life who's able to do what he likes with me!']

Norah was responsible for the staff of the Welsh department and Carwyn, of course, needed a lot of time off to pursue his rugby interests. He'd seen how best to make that happen and it was easy enough to buy 'a little something' for Norah in order to get the time off needed.

I must mention our captain on that tour, John Dawes, the London Welsh centre. Without doubt, one of the best captains I've ever played with. He was never regarded as a star like some of the other 1970s players. But he was extremely talented and always consistent. His fellow players could always depend on him and, as a captain, he excelled. Like Barry John, he thought about the game in a similar way to Carwyn.

Out in New Zealand, it's a forwards' game more than anything. Carwyn's message to us was: 'Boys, if we can get 45 per cent of the ball, we can beat them!'

When the forwards won possession, there was no shortage of talent amongst our backs to make good use of it. To return to Carwyn's point about playing to the weaknesses of the opposition, he decided that the All Blacks full back, Fergie McCormick, was a weak link in their team. Gareth, Barry and JPR were instructed to kick towards him at every opportunity. He, in turn, had a nightmare of a time, with Barry particularly making a fool of him.

Carwyn was more than aware of our weaknesses, too. He held many a session concentrating on weak areas in any individual player's game. If one of the backs, for example, was naturally a right-footed player, he'd spend a lot of time making that player kick with his left foot. Likewise, with someone passing the ball: if they were better passing to their right, he'd work on their left-hand-side passing.

We were really lucky with the players who travelled to New Zealand in 1971. Many of the Welsh players in their midst were starting to shine, showing the success that was to become a feature of their play throughout the 1970s. However, players from other countries too were at the top of their game in New Zealand: David Duckham from England, for one, and Mike Gibson from Ireland. We did achieve a historical feat of course, winning a Test series on New Zealand soil for the first time ever. That was a special, incredible feeling, a proud moment in my career.

It's strange how some people are so ready to judge, even in the midst of success. Many tried to find a way to play the whole thing down and Carwyn was usually at the butt end of those comments. It was no wonder they won, the detractors would say, looking at the talented players Carwyn James had at his disposal – anyone could coach talent like that. That was extremely unfair and an immature reaction from people who should have known better. The rugby world knew full well the length and breadth of Carwyn's achievement. New Zealand rugby still says to this day that the 1971 Lions tour was a major contribution to the development of the game in their country. They say that, knowing that they as a nation hate losing and really feel pain on the rare occasions when they lose. Without a doubt, they were shaken in 1971. But they soon showed their appreciation of what was achieved by Carwyn and his squad. Graham Henry, during his time as Wales coach, would often refer to the importance of Carwyn's contribution to the game in New Zealand, and to him personally too, as he considered whether to be a rugby coach himself.

The fact that no Lions team has achieved the feat of winning a Test series in New Zealand since then, says a lot, too. But if anyone still persisted in finding faults, their mouths were firmly shut the following year when Carwyn was responsible for yet another famous victory over the mighty All Blacks.

11

Bells

IF ANYONE WERE to ask me – and actually, many have – which was the best day of my life as a rugby player, I'd say categorically, 31 October 1972. That was the day, in case you weren't sure, that Llanelli defeated the All Blacks at Stradey Park. It was the biggest day of my life up until then and nothing has bettered it since, with my now having passed three score years and ten. I must emphasise that that was my best day on a rugby field! I'm sure that my wedding day would have to be the best day overall, although it would be very difficult to separate the two!

I first learned that the All Blacks would be coming to play Llanelli during the New Zealand trip with the Lions in 1971. In one of those regular chats between Carwyn and the Welsh boys, Carwyn told Derek Quinnell and myself, the two Llanelli players on the tour, that the All Blacks had been invited to play in Llanelli on their next tour of the British Isles. Well, it was quite difficult to know how to react. I was really excited to think that we'd be playing such a world rugby power in our own back yard. And hearing this news, out there in their midst, made it all the more exciting. Once we'd beaten New Zealand in the Test series and once that news had sunk in, I could turn my attention to the fact that I'd be playing them again soon, but this time with my Llanelli team-mates.

On our return after the Lions tour, there wasn't that much focus on the impending All Blacks visit. Not all the players knew about it, and there was no need to inform them that early on. I've no doubt that Carwyn and the committee members were very busy with arrangements. But the news didn't filter through to many of the players until a few months before the All Blacks arrived. In my case, and the other international players at Stradey, we had the 1972 Five Nations to think about first.

That was certainly a very different Five Nations Championship. I played in every game, but I only played three games. That sounds like material for a pub quiz, and indeed it is! The explanation is that the Championship wasn't completed that year for the first time since the Second World War. Neither the Wales team nor the Scotland team were prepared to travel to play their matches in Ireland. It had been a bad year in the political and military troubles of Northern Ireland and players were concerned about their safety. That was the year of the horrors of Bloody Sunday, when many Northern Irish people were killed by British soldiers. It was a particularly volatile period in an increasingly unstable situation.

Consequently, the last international we played in the 1972 Five Nations was against France on 25 March. We won comfortably enough, 20–6, following tries by John Bevan and Gerald Davies, with four penalties from the boot of Barry John. We didn't know it at the time, but those were the last points Barry would score for Wales and the last time he pulled on a Welsh jersey. What a loss he was to Welsh rugby.

Barry did play one more time in Wales, and at Cardiff Arms Park, too. He played in a star-studded game to commemorate the 50th anniversary of the Urdd, the Welsh League of Youth. Carwyn James was asked to pick a XV and Barry was asked to choose the opposing XV. In the end, it turned out to be almost a Lions side (Carwyn's), minus its Welsh players, against a Wales side (Barry's) which included its Lions. Barry's team wore green and included nine Lions from the 1971 tour. When I turned up at the ground to play for Barry's team, I was told that the Wales international and Lions prop, John Lloyd from Bridgend, had pulled out, so once again I ended up playing prop. I was up against the Scottish Lion, Sandy Carmichael, and what a challenge that was! Gareth and Barry were our halfbacks, of course, and Phil Bennett and Chico Hopkins were Carwyn's halfbacks. The latter were to play 9 and 10 in the same team again later on that year, although at the time they played for two different clubs.

The Urdd game was on a Wednesday evening, with a 6.15 p.m. kick-off. There were over 30,000 there to watch what was bound to be an exciting match. No-one had any idea, however, that it would be Barry's very last game of rugby. When that fact became evident some time later, the Urdd event became even more special. And, of course, as a man with a sense of occasion, Barry scored a try that night, one that was typical of his style of play. He ran about 40 yards, weaving in and out of tackles as if they weren't there, much to the crowd's rapturous delight.

But don't ask me who won; I've no idea. That wasn't important that night. It was a unique opportunity for the fans to see many of the victorious 1971 Lions. It was a fantastic opportunity for the Urdd to raise money to support the wonderful work they do. No-one would have been more proud of an opportunity to do so than Carwyn himself. The match programme is full of contributions from many of the greats of Welsh rugby – people such as Dewi Bebb, Onllwyn Brace and Cliff Morgan. All three praised the contribution that the Urdd had made to the lives of youngsters in Wales.

Some weeks later, I was back in Cardiff with Llanelli for the first ever Welsh Cup final. It was a brand-new competition that had captured the imagination of the rugby public, and an indication of how the game was developing in Wales at the time. Unfortunately, we lost to Neath. But we'd be back there for many more finals in the following years and we'd win every one of them.

The 1971/72 season drew to a close in a very upbeat manner. However, as the new season approached, our minds began to turn to the fact that the All Blacks would be coming to town in October. Carwyn had obviously started to think about whom he wanted to select to play against the tourists. However, before any decisions could be made, Llanelli had the small matter of an overseas tour – to South Africa. Once again, Carwyn stuck to his guns and refused to go with the team. Norman Gale took charge of the tour, with Phil Bennett as captain.

I did go on that tour, even though I'd been quite upset by the things I'd seen when I was there with the Lions. My feeling was that I was going out there to play rugby, but also that those experiences I'd had that time had proved there was a way for us rugby players to express what our thoughts about the situation were.

But, what worried me most while I was preparing to go out there was actually the thought of giving up rugby completely. I'd started to think about that after returning from the Lions tour in 1971. There were many reasons for thoughts of retirement: I'd been on three British Lions tours, had experienced a Lions Test series win in New Zealand, and had won the Grand Slam with Wales. I'd had a fantastic time with Llanelli, and had been there when Carwyn James was transforming the club and the rugby it played. What more could I achieve? It was probably best to start thinking in terms of the end approaching, as things wouldn't get any better than this for me on a rugby pitch.

Off the field, my family situation had also changed. At the end of the 1960s, I'd met a young girl from Carmarthen at a dance in the Barracks on one of my Saturday night journeys out of Bancyfelin. We got married at St Peter's Church in the town, as my wife-to-be, Bethan, was a member there and sang in the choir. She worked in the Ministry of Agriculture offices at the time. After the wedding there was no opportunity for us to go on an overseas honeymoon; we had a three-day break in Llandudno, because I'd promised to play for the Irish Wolfhounds in Dublin. We got married on a Saturday, spent a few days in Llandudno until Wednesday, and then returned to Carmarthen so that I could fly out to Ireland. Once again, I had to take time off work – three days to get married and the rest for the rugby. That must have been difficult for Bethan to accept, but it was an early indication of what life as a rugby player's wife was going to be like.

We'd been married for three years before our first child, Tracy, was born in 1971. Having decided to start a family, we'd planned to change the pattern of our family life. One central consideration, as far as that was concerned, was holidays. To go abroad with the rugby, for Llanelli, Wales or the Lions, meant taking time off work, meaning that there was little time left to be with the family. If we were going to have children there would therefore be no holiday time for me with them.

On the family front, I had a bitter blow when I returned from New Zealand in 1971. Bethan came to meet me at Carmarthen railway station with our first-born, Tracy. The little one stayed away from me, as she was afraid of this 'strange man'. I'd been away from home for five months and she had no idea who I was. Back home, the three of us were sat in the living room. When Bethan left the room, Tracy hurried out after her mother as fast as she could, not wanting to be alone in the room with me. That shook me to the core and I vowed never to be away from home for very long periods again.

Having decided that I'd go to South Africa therefore, I also vowed to tell the club that I was retiring as soon as we got back home. And yes, that was despite the fact that I knew that the All Blacks were on the way. However, I was the one who was to receive a big surprise.

On the plane home from South Africa, the club chairman, Handel Greville, came to talk to me. Quite simply, the club wanted me to be the captain for the forthcoming season, which meant, of course, that I'd captain Llanelli against the All Blacks. Although he wasn't on the plane, Carwyn's hand was firmly behind all this, I sensed. It was a massive shock. I hadn't been captain for the season that had just ended. I wasn't captain for the tour of South Africa. But they now wanted me to be captain. Handel said that the proposal was to be put to the other players first to see if they approved. He did so, right there on the plane. As soon as he shared what he proposed, Grav jumped onto his feet to second the proposal. I wonder if he was following Carwyn's instructions. Everybody backed the idea so, by the time I stepped off the plane, I was the captain of Llanelli Rugby Club for the season ahead. The club had decided that the 1972/73 season would be its centenary season, too.

There's been a great deal of discussion since as to the accuracy of that, but it was accepted at the time, and it was a year full of centenary celebration events. And into all this came the visit of the All Blacks. I'd be leading my players out on the field at Stradey to play the best team in the world. That hadn't entered my mind when Carwyn had told Derek and I about the tour back in New Zealand. But I wonder whether that was an idea in Carwyn's mind at the time, long before the date of the match?

12

Raw Eggs and Sherry

As soon as we returned from South Africa, the focus turned to playing the All Blacks in October. Most of the players had realised by then that there was a big fixture ahead of them in the new season, although some didn't really register that fact until the season began properly. However, the game against the All Blacks did increase in its prominence as time went on. There would be conversations here and there about it, the club would announce some detail about the arrangements for the occasion, and we'd hear some mention of it outside the club occasionally. I'm sure that Carwyn thought about this game more than anything else, but he didn't divulge that to us at the start of the season.

Carwyn obviously thought it necessary to strengthen the squad. He made it known that he wanted three new players to add to the strength of the squad. Over a period of a few months, from midsummer right up until a few weeks before the game, he approached three specific players and asked them to join Llanelli. He succeeded in getting all three: winger JJ Williams from Bridgend, scrum half Chico Hopkins from Maesteg, and flanker Tom David from Pontypridd. All three said that they agreed to join the club having been impressed with what Carwyn was achieving there. Llanelli, they said, was the team to play for if you had an ounce of ambition, because they were the Man U of the rugby world.

By the start of October Carwyn had his squad in place. He was able to choose who he wanted because of an agreement he had with the club committee. He'd asked for the right to have control over his players, which included team selection. The committee has to be praised for understanding Carwyn's vision and giving him the freedom to follow it. After all, it was that committee who had the vision to invite Carwyn to be coach in the first place.

In the weeks before the game, Carwyn arranged for local village teams to play against us on training nights. A week before the game he took us up to Gloucester to watch the All Blacks play Western Counties in their first game of the tour. Both these arrangements show that Carwyn was thinking differently from others about rugby coaching.

That was also evident when it came time to choose the team that would face the All Blacks at Stradey. Although responsible for selections, Carwyn asked his assistant, former international hooker and forwards' coach Norman Gale, to help in the process, and also myself as captain. But we didn't meet to discuss selections in one of the rooms at Stradey, we met at Carwyn's home in Cefneithin. We had a relatively informal chat in his living room, where the downfall of the mighty All Blacks was plotted. It was a fairly straightforward process but two positions caused me some particular grief personally.

Llanelli's popular scrum half at the time was Selwyn Williams. He was an excellent player, lively around the pitch and always a handful for the opposition, especially when his colourful language could be heard! But Carwyn had brought Chico Hopkins in from Maesteg. Carwyn thought that Chico had more big-match experience than Selwyn, as he had a Wales cap and was part of the 1971 tour. Similarly, Alan James was an excellent flanker for Llanelli, a loyal servant and a hard player. But Carwyn had brought Tom David from Pontypridd, because Tom offered more of a ball-carrying ability than Alan and he could run at his opponents. Tom was chosen, as was Chico. I have absolutely nothing against either of the players brought in. It isn't a criticism of them. However, I must say that both those decisions were really tough ones for me, especially dropping Selwyn. I still feel bad about that. To his credit, he took it very well and he's been honourable in the way he's discussed it since that day. But in my opinion, he should have played.

Having chosen the team, Phil Bennett joined us and we all left Carwyn's house to head towards Llandeilo. In his usual style, Carwyn had booked a table for us at the Angel in Salem. Over food and a bottle of wine, we discussed the forthcoming game and our approach to it.

Llanelli itself was also beginning to get ready for

the grand arrival. Two shop windows in the town centre were filled with photographs and posters related to Llanelli and New Zealand rugby, with one poster announcing clearly in bold letters, 'The All Blacks are coming!' A flowerbed was planted in the grounds of the town hall, marking the centenary of the club, and columns of the local newspaper, *The Llanelli Star*, were filled every week with stories about the forthcoming game. There was a strong sense of excitement and expectancy in the town and the surrounding area, which was nice to be a part of. It was quite special how the town had caught on to this visit and was very much a part of the whole build-up and occasion. I'm sure that some of this expectancy resulted from what Carwyn was achieving at the club, and the local people wanted to buy into it. A visit from one of the three southern hemisphere teams didn't happen that often and that gave such a visit greater importance and significance. It was the first time in nearly ten years that the New Zealanders had come to town and the whole area wanted to make sure they received a big, warm, Welsh welcome.

And then, after much anticipation and preparation, the morning of the game arrived. I woke fairly early. I'd arranged a lift with Roy Bergiers, who also lived in Carmarthen. Off we went in his Wolseley towards Llanelli. We were all to meet up at the team hotel, the Ashburnham, in Burry Port. Such an idea was also new and a Carwyn innovation. He wanted us to meet away from Stradey and travel to the ground together by coach. That happens all the time now, of course, but it didn't then.

Around mid-morning we all had a meal together. When it comes to pre-match meals, every player has his own routine. Some didn't want to eat at all, some ate a little, while others had everything that was on offer. That included our full back, Roger Davies. He was a student at Trinity College, Carmarthen, at the time and his attitude was simple – as a student, if there was a free meal on offer, he had to eat everything! For my part, before big games, I had a routine of breaking two raw eggs into a glass of sherry and downing it in one. The two youngest players in the team, Ray Gravell and Gareth Jenkins, saw me do this and thought that it must be a good thing to do as I'd been on three Lions tours! After looking at each other bemusedly, they did the same thing. I don't think it went down as well with them as it did with me, judging by their faces anyway!

Carwyn had arranged for some people to call round to see us at the Ashburnham. The club chairman, Handel Greville, came to speak to us, as did the coaching manager of the WRU, Ray Williams. Carwyn noticed that we were all getting a little bit too worked up too soon. So, he took us out of the hotel for a walk, across the road to the Ashburnham Golf Club, where we'd had a meeting the night before. By the time we all got back to the hotel, we were relaxed once more and Carwyn's tactic had worked.

It was my turn then to talk to the players. It's strange how time plays tricks with the mind. When there was an opportunity in 2012 to mark 40 years since the All Blacks game, there was disagreement amongst the boys as to where I delivered the speech. Some said that it was at the Ashburnham, others that it was at Stradey, and some said both. I was convinced that I spoke to the boys at the hotel. Following those discussions in 2012, I now think that I gave my main speech at the hotel but also said a few additional words in the dressing room at Stradey. So everybody's right!

The other players have been kind enough to tell me personally, and to say publicly too, that my speech inspired them. Phil Bennett told the *Western Mail* as much, and the headline the following day was, 'Brilliant Delme talk had me in tears'. That wasn't my intention. What I tried to do, as I stood in front of the boys, was to give them an idea of what victory that day would mean to me personally. I told them that I'd been on three Lions tours and had won the Grand Slam with Wales, but would be willing to give all that up if we could beat the All Blacks on our own ground in front of our own people. Those who would be there watching us that day, I said, were the people of the town and the surrounding villages throughout Carmarthenshire. They were the people who worked side by side with us in the steelworks, the schools, the local authority, and so on. For me, winning in front of these people would mean more than anything else, yes, even more than winning a Test series out in New Zealand.

I went on to say that achieving such a victory

wouldn't be easy. It would require total commitment, stubbornness, and a physicality that hadn't been shown before. On many occasions before that day I'd told the players that they hadn't played rugby until they'd played the All Blacks. I was always derided and teased for saying that. But at the Ashburnham I said the same thing again. I told them they would be tackled harder and more ferociously than ever before; the play wouldn't be pretty or clean, either. But, if they could read the match report of the game in the *Western Mail* the following day, then that meant that they'd succeeded in lasting out until the end of the game, even if they couldn't remember much about it.

Then it was time to get on the bus; we travelled through the Burry Port streets and towards Llanelli. It was unbelievable to see crowds of people standing on the pavements cheering us on our way, with scarves and banners waving. Not one of us had seen anything like it, not even the most experienced international or Lion. When we stepped off the bus into the middle of hordes at Stradey Park, it was even more unbelievable. We couldn't move for ages.

When we finally got into our changing room, we sat down at our usual places. The word then got around that the All Blacks' bus had arrived. Many of the boys stood on the changing room benches to peep out of the long window high above them. The All Blacks created quite an impression as they stepped off their bus. The senior players were wearing the cowboy hats they'd bought in Canada

on their way over to Britain – these elder statesmen
had more of a Mafia look about them than chapel
elders! They were criticised for wearing those hats
by their supporters back home; they said it gave an
unfavourable impression of New Zealand rugby.

However, our players weren't standing looking out
through the window for long. Carwyn soon put a stop
to that. He asked everyone to sit down, saying that
he wasn't keen for us to concentrate too much on the
opposition. He then escorted me out onto the pitch,
so that I could sample the atmosphere there and get
an idea of what Stradey looked like beforehand. It
was an incredible sight. By the time the whole team
arrived on the pitch for a photograph, it was even
more remarkable a sight. There were supporters
everywhere, in every nook and cranny, and so close
to the pitch. If there are many versions as to where I
gave my pre-match speech, there are also very many
accounts of how many people were in the ground to
watch the game that day. Figures range from 18,000
to 28,000. Moreover, if you believe everyone who says
they were at the game, the total attendance would
be half the population of Carmarthenshire! The
truth is that there were about 25,000 present. That's
according to Marlston Morgan, the friend who sat
with me under the clock at Paddington on the day
I heard I'd been selected for the Lions. By 1972 he
was on the Llanelli committee and responsible for
the press and ticketing that day.

As a result of so many being in the ground, Carwyn
didn't keep us out there for too long, in case it all got

too much for us too soon. We went back inside and there was a chance for me to say a few words again. But only after Grav had been through his usual pre-match routine though – he'd grab a toilet roll, go to the toilet and be sick, rather loudly. Then he'd bang his head violently against the toilet door before starting to sing some songs at the top of his voice. He did that for every game and it would be no different on the day he faced the All Blacks.

I didn't say much in the changing room. But it seemed to have an effect similar to the speech at the Ashburnham. Grav and Gareth Jenkins both said that, after hearing me, they were prepared to walk out onto the pitch through the wall instead of the door! We did leave for the pitch, through the door, ready to face the biggest game of our lives.

13

Victory

It's impossible to describe what it was like to walk out into the cauldron that was Stradey Park that day. The impact of leaving the tunnel and stepping out on the field in front of 25,000 enthusiastic and vocal fans was substantial. The All Blacks felt the same. Their winger that day, Bryan Williams, who is now president of New Zealand Rugby Union, said that the crowd size and noise shook them as players, especially when they realised they were so close to the pitch. He also noted one other thing that seemed threatening to them as visitors – the fact that the scoreboard was in Welsh. He said it made them feel like strangers and made them uncomfortable.

We had a fantastic start to the game. Within the first five minutes, they'd given away a penalty following an infringement at a line-out. Carwyn's coaching sessions had concentrated a lot on the line-out, as he perceived it to be one of their weaknesses. Within a matter of minutes, he was proved right. Phil Bennett took the penalty kick from a fair distance out. The ball hit the post and bounced back into the field of play. Their scrum half, Lindsay

Colling, caught it and went to kick it downfield, but our centre, Roy Bergiers, charged the kick down, chased the ball over the line and grounded it for a try. A dramatic start to the game without a doubt, and one that sent the crowd wild. The scoreboard read: Llanelli 6 Seland Newydd 0.

If you speak to most of the players today, I don't think many of them would remember much else about the game. I doubt if any of the moves or passages of play have stayed in the memory. But we all remember that it wasn't a very clean game. The word brutal has been used and I won't disagree with that. Some things have stayed in the mind, such as a great tackle by Roger Davies; a run by Chico Hopkins; Barry Llywelyn, the prop, keeping their Alistair Scown very quiet throughout the game; Gareth Jenkins throwing himself at everybody with no care for his own well-being and, of course, Andy Hill's kick that put us 9–3 ahead.

But there is one move above all others that has stayed with almost all the boys on the pitch that day. It was towards the end of the game and the All Blacks were pressing very hard to try and win the game. They kicked the ball right back into the corner near our tryline, a beautiful kick. Phil Bennett was there to gather the ball but he had very little room to manoeuvre and, on top of that, their wing, Grant Batty, was bearing down on him. Somehow, Phil caught the ball, turned on a sixpence, and put in a downfield kick that flew into their half. As it soared through the air, it spun out more and more towards the touchline and their full back, Kirwan, had to run out to try to catch it. The pressure on us had been lifted by a piece of magic from Benny. But the lasting image of that move is of Grant Batty flying through the air to tackle Phil, but Phil's sidestep was so quick and skilful that he wasn't there to be tackled and Batty landed flat on his face in the mud! The crowd was delighted. Some years later, Grant Batty was enough of a man to admit that Phil had been brilliant in that manoeuvre and that he really was made a fool of.

As the game drew to a close we had a six-point lead, but it was still difficult to think in terms of us winning. I began to believe that we might win after Phil's magical clearance. Thankfully, we did manage to hold on to our lead and the final whistle heralded our victory. We'd beaten the All Blacks!

Stradey went completely bonkers. The pitch was drowned in a sea of fans and I was lifted up onto the shoulders of some of them. Some tried to lift Roy Bergiers, but they made a mess of it and he landed on his backside on the pitch, with his legs up in the air. It took an absolute age for us to reach the changing room and, once we got there, that too was full to the brim. Grown men were crying in there, we were hugged by one and all, some took mud from our boots as a souvenir, even! Everybody was singing, smiling, laughing, cheering. And, in the midst of it all, Carwyn, smiling from ear to ear, quietly pleased and proud. There wasn't a murmur from the other changing room. It was like a mortuary.

The post-match dinner was held in the Patrons'
Room above the changing rooms. It was total
pandemonium there, too. It must have been a very
difficult place for the All Blacks squad to be. Many
of our boys tell stories of blunt responses from some
All Blacks to attempts at conversation during dinner.
One of our boys stood next to Sid Going in the gents,
and he asked him politely how he was. The answer
came back in two words, the second being 'off'.

Gareth Jenkins has one of the best stories of that
day. As I said, he threw himself at everything and
everyone in the game and he walked off the field with
two big, black eyes. A man came up to him – who
Gareth didn't know – and congratulated him on his
performance. He then turned to Gareth and gave him
a £10 note, telling him that the best cure for black
eyes was to put a thick slice of steak on them. The
money was offered so that Gareth could buy steak.
However, Gareth saw things differently. He worked
in the Klondike steelworks at that time and his wage
was just over £20 a week. He, therefore, had half his
weekly wage in his hands in order to buy meat to put
on his black eyes. No way, he thought, as he walked
towards the bar to celebrate. That money paid for
Gareth to have the following day off work.

After the dinner, there was a function at the
Glen Ballroom, in Llanelli's town centre. There was
more food there and entertainment for us, too. I
didn't remember who entertained us until some of
the boys mentioned it during the 40th anniversary
celebrations. Singing and sharing their jokes were

Ryan and Ronnie, the popular double act. They were beginning their period of stardom, having performed a lot in Welsh up until then, and that year they started to perform in English, too. What a great shame that we were all so caught up in the joys of celebrating our win that we couldn't even appreciate who was on stage!

After the Glen, we all went back to the place where our day together had begun, the Ashburnham Hotel. That's where we stayed, talking and socialising, until the early hours of the morning. No-one wanted to leave. But, I left about 3 a.m. as I had to be at work by 8 a.m. As I walked into the office that morning, everyone shared in my joy, saying they were all extremely proud. My boss asked me what on the earth I was doing back in work, why didn't I take the day off? My reply was that's what I was supposed to do and that's how it should be. Many of the boys hadn't had permission to have time off to play the game, and others had time off but without pay. Our try scorer, Roy Bergiers, for example, was given time off but without pay, only to realise later that his fellow teachers and a good number of pupils were at the game, the staff being there on full pay. So they were paid to watch *him* play (without reimbursement) against the All Blacks!

The press came to my workplace the following morning, too. A photograph of me, reading the account of the game in the morning's newspaper, was taken. The attention, as a result of that victory, was something I'd have to learn to get used to.

The response to the victory was overwhelming to be honest. That famous saying about pubs running dry after the match is just one of the stories which has gone into rugby folklore. The news of the victory spread like wildfire throughout Wales. One man was largely responsible for that, the legendary Max Boyce. Two days after the game, he'd composed a song about our triumph which would help keep the memory of the day alive: '9–3' was one of his early popular songs, with immortal lines such as '… and the beer flowed at Stradey, pumped down from Felinfoel!' The game was important for the Grogg empire, too. The creator of the popular clay creatures, John Hughes, was at the game with his son. The victory was decisive in their move away from producing mythical clay creatures to ones based on real rugby players. I was lucky enough to have a Grogg based on me quite early on. I have both arms in the air, fists clenched, just as I was when carried off the pitch that famous day.

There's no doubt that the match caught the imagination of people outside the Llanelli area, too. Other teams from Wales had beaten the All Blacks, but without such a triumphal response throughout the rest of Wales. I'm not too sure why that would be. But I do know why we as players were so determined and focused that day. Firstly, we all believed, in advance of the day of the match, that we could win. That became clear when we travelled to Gloucester to see them play a few days before our game. We didn't see anything that made us think they could beat us.

Carwyn believed that firmly too and he said so on our return from Gloucester. Not all the players could go to see that game, Phil Bennett being one. He was there at Stradey to meet us when we returned and he says that he couldn't get over how confident we were, how strong our belief was that we could beat them. Most teams who lose to the All Blacks lose before they get on the pitch, they've lost the mental battle. We were ready for them as we walked out onto the Stradey pitch on 31 October. We didn't feel that they were a threat, even if we did feel their hits!

Added to this was the influence of Carwyn James, of course. He'd orchestrated the defeat of the All Blacks in their own country just over a year earlier. And even though some tried to take that success away from him, he'd managed to do the same again, this time with his club. We all felt so pleased for him. That silenced his detractors once and for all. Not that Carwyn was the type of person to think like that, but we were.

And then, through all that, there was a strong conviction among many of us that the victory came from the very roots of the club itself, which had been established by John Rogers, a man who'd had a private education at Rugby School. He'd come to Llanelli and established steelworks in the town. Rugby became a game for the working man almost immediately in Llanelli. The link between the game, the club and the area's heavy industries is long and deep. It's back to that kind of work many of us went the Monday after the weekend game, week in, week out. That's where we'd be given our colleagues' opinion of the team and our own performance. The Saturday afternoon game was a ritual followed to unwind after the graft of the working week. As we played, it was these men, latterly the women too, who stood on the terraces around us.

The significance of the 1972 victory was that it was working men and women from the area who had achieved and witnessed it. That's why this victory, in my own square mile, in front of my own people, was worth more to me than anything else I've achieved on the rugby fields of the world. My words at the Ashburnham Hotel were not empty words.

14

Rest

IT's VERY DIFFICULT to remember anything else from that 1972/73 season to be honest. There was plenty going on, of course, as it was the centenary year and many functions were arranged to mark that anniversary. Other events were organised to celebrate the All Blacks victory, too. However, things would never be the same once we'd beaten the New Zealanders. Playing against them is an honour, defeating them even more of an honour. I played against them eleven times but only beat them twice, with one drawn match. You have to treasure victories as rare as that.

As individual players we were invited to many a function to speak to particular groups, in clubs and societies all across south Wales. On the pitch we played some special matches to mark the centenary. We beat the Barbarians, for example, but you don't hear much about that game any more. I was also given the privilege of being the captain of the Wales team who played the All Blacks on 2 December 1972. It was a really good feeling, walking out on the pitch at the Arms Park, leading the team which represented my country. The game was very close, and we nearly beat them. They won in the end, 19–16. Five of the boys who beat them at Stradey played in the Wales team that day.

Llanelli's season ended in a good way. We reached the final of the Welsh Cup again, where Cardiff were our opponents. We played really well in the five games leading up to the final, scoring over 150 points, conceding only 15. Our hopes were high that we'd clinch our first Welsh Cup at the Arms Park. Many complained that, as the final was held in Cardiff, our opponents were in effect playing at home. But the game went ahead in the capital and we won comfortably, 30–7. It was a great end to a magnificent season. It was also the beginning of a long unbeaten Cup run, with our fans getting an annual day out in Cardiff!

At the end of the season, a lavish centenary dinner was held in a huge marquee erected on the pitch at Stradey. Stars from the rugby world were there, as well as those associated with the club. There was one more milestone left for us before we could officially say goodbye to that remarkable season – a rugby tour of Canada.

Carwyn once more wanted to make his mark on that aspect of club life. He asked the committee if it would be all right for the wives and girlfriends of players to come on tour, too. That was as revolutionary as anything Carwyn did at the club! It was traditionally, categorically, only men who travelled anywhere in the name of the club. But

Carwyn believed that the women played an integral part in the club's success and that they should be rewarded for their support.

He'd included partners in one of the events before the Cup final, too. One Sunday afternoon he took the squad to Llandovery College for a training session. When we'd finished, we were to go to Plas Glansevin nearby, a very popular place to go to in the 1970s. Traditional Welsh medieval evenings were held there, and *cawl* (Welsh broth) and mead flowed in equal measure. When we got there, our wives and girlfriends were already waiting for us. We had a fantastic evening, where we all relaxed and enjoyed each other's company. Carwyn arranged the first round of drinks for everyone. However, when that was all gone, there was some uncertainty as to whether we'd be allowed a second drink and, if so, who'd pay for it. Carwyn said there was no problem and we should carry on ordering, the drinks were on the house. Carwyn took the bill to the committee the following week and he was rigorously questioned about the expenditure. Carwyn's considered response was that it was all in the name of preparing the club for the Cup final. They should, he said, come back to him after the final if they still thought that the money wasn't well spent. No further word was heard about the Glansevin bill.

The committee then agreed to Carwyn's request that wives and girlfriends should be allowed to go on the tour of Canada. Naturally, the ladies were delighted. When I mention Carwyn's name today,

Bethan always responds by saying, 'Oh, marvellous man!' Carwyn was teased quite a bit by a few of the players when they learned that the wives would be allowed to go. 'Why the hell do we have to bring the missus?' was their cry. Carwyn would simply smile back in response. Players and officials from other clubs certainly gave us a hard time because of the women's presence in Canada, with many making fun of us!

The Llanelli ladies responded positively to the decision to take them on tour and they held many fundraising events towards the costs of their trip. Bethan, for example, was involved in organising a fashion show. It was a very successful evening and I'm sure it must have been one of the first fashion events held in the name of a rugby club. The show certainly created quite a stir among rugby clubs when they heard about it. In order for Bethan to come with me, Tracy had to stay with her grandmother in Bancyfelin. Thank goodness such support was possible. We left for Canada, all the money collected and our wives by our sides.

Not all the boys had a wife or girlfriend, of course. The single boys thought it was a very strange set-up for them to be in. But, to their credit, they fitted in well with it all and if anything was an issue they didn't show it. It was as much a change of world for them as it was for us to take our wives. For two of the players, it was a very special trip indeed. Roger Davies had just got married and, a few days earlier, so had Hefin Jenkins. The tour was both couples' honeymoon, therefore. Marlston Morgan, who was with us on the tour, heard that Hefin and his new wife had been given a room with two single beds. Fair play to him and his wife, they swapped room with Hefin so that they could have a double bed. It wasn't all about rugby.

This was my second visit to Canada that summer. Wales had been out there a few weeks earlier. It was early days for rugby in Canada. The game had been played there for a number of years but, as far as stepping onto the world stage was concerned, they really were only starting out. Llanelli and Wales won every game in Canada that year. I'd lost once in Canada, of course, on that Lions tour of 1966, when sunburn cost us the game! Canada have come on in leaps and bounds since those early days, and it's great to see that.

When I returned from the Llanelli tour of Canada I was absolutely determined this time that I'd retire from the game. I'd decided that before going there and nothing would change my mind this time around. I informed the club that I was giving up the game and that my playing days were over. I did find it difficult to give up completely, so I played a few games for Carmarthen Athletic.

Each Boxing Day, the tradition at the Athletic was for the team to play a team of former players. That year I was chosen to play for the Athletic second XV. However, Llanelli had its own Boxing Day tradition, playing London Welsh at Stradey, always a big occasion and a real community event. I received a last-minute call to play for Llanelli in their game. I had a problem, therefore. Who to play for? In the end I played the first half for the Athletic seconds in the morning, and then raced over to Stradey to play for Llanelli in the afternoon. I shouldn't have played two games on the same day really, but I didn't feel I could pull out of one game and I couldn't turn down the other.

Following that Boxing Day Llanelli appearance, I was asked to play a few more games between then and the end of the season. That led to another really unexpected game for Wales, too. My last international was against England in the 1974 Five Nations Championship. That was the only time I lost to England. Perhaps I shouldn't have ventured back to Stradey that Boxing Day; I'd have kept my 100 per cent record against the old enemy then!

I did give the game up completely at the end of the 1974 season. A year later, our second child Helen was born. That meant that we could spend a lot of time together as a family of four. I had to adjust to life without rugby and that was made so much easier by having a strong family. I don't know where I would be without them. And that brings us back full circle to where my story started. I found dealing with that change really difficult and it cost me. Maybe now you understand the heights from which I fell, a little more clearly. To go from all that, to nothing, made me break down.

But I'm not in that situation now. I'm enjoying my life and my family. I look back with great pleasure and delight at the career I had in rugby. I enjoyed 15 good years. I'm also very glad that I played the game in those days and not today. When I played I also had a career outside sport. There was variety to the pattern of my life and I was more a part of my community. And none of that hindered what I was able to achieve on the field, either.

I still watch rugby matches every weekend, on the television – mainly Scarlets games, but not exclusively. I still follow Welsh rugby as passionately as ever. But as far as watching live rugby is concerned, I do that in Carmarthen these days, going to see either the Quins or the Athletic play. I really enjoy seeing young talent develop through clubs, such as these two in my home town.

After all the travelling I did as a rugby player, to many fascinating and beautiful countries, I can still say to this day that all that did was to make me appreciate the old saying even more – there's no place like home!

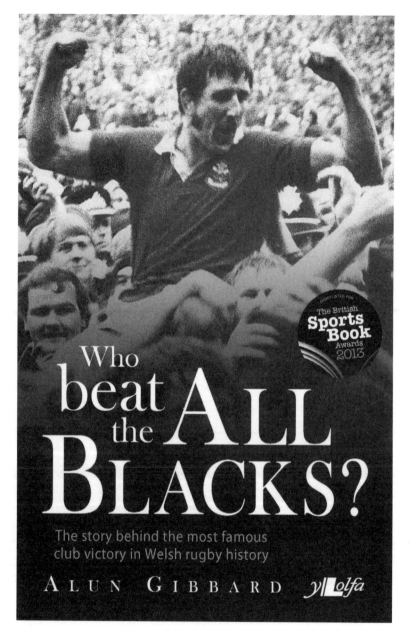

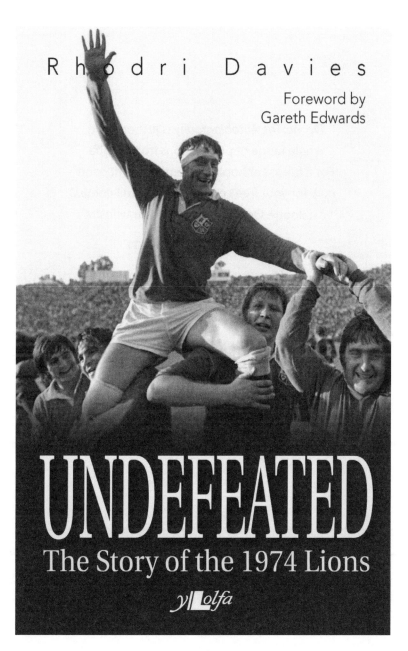

R h o d r i   D a v i e s

Foreword by
Gareth Edwards

UNDEFEATED
The Story of the 1974 Lions

y Lolfa

£9.95

Delme: The Autobiography is just one of a
whole range of publications from Y Lolfa.
For a full list of books currently in print, send
now for your free copy of our new full-colour
catalogue. Or simply surf into our website

www.ylolfa.com

for secure on-line ordering.

TALYBONT CEREDIGION CYMRU SY24 5HE
e-mail ylolfa@ylolfa.com
website www.ylolfa.com
phone (01970) 832 304
fax 832 782